D0513663

How to Spot a B*st*rd by his Starsign

HOW TO SPOT A B*ST*RD
BY HIS STAR SIGN

The Ultimate Horrorscope

ADELE LANG AND SUSI RAJAH

MAINSTREAM
PUBLISHING

EDINBURGH AND LONDON

Copyright – Adèle Lang and Susi Rajah, 1997

All rights reserved

The moral rights of the authors have been asserted

First published in Great Britain in 1997 by
MAINSTREAM PUBLISHING COMPANY (EDINBURGH) LTD
7 Albany Street
Edinburgh EH1 3UG

First published in 1996 in Australia by Pan Macmillan Australia Pty Limited

ISBN 1 85158 948 1

No part of this book may be reproduced or transmitted in any form or by any means
without written permission from the publisher, except by a reviewer who wishes to
quote brief passages in connection with a review written for insertion in a magazine,
newspaper or broadcast

A catalogue record for this book is available from the British Library

Typeset in Berkeley
Printed and bound in Finland by WSOY

In memory of Rosemary Thewliss, the Pisces with the strength of Hercules. Give Saint Peter hell.

Acknowledgements

Thanks to Linda Goodman whose kind words inspired us to set the record straight. Rest in peace, fellow fire sign.

Thanks to family, friends, colleagues and mentors, past and present, for their blind faith, long-suffering sighs and occasionally useful astrological anecdotes: Michael Andrews, Denis Bernar, Jon Bird, Rose Bisignano, Tim Brierley, Scott Bundy, Fiona Burton, Leesa Candeloro, John Cecil, Terry Cheverton, Trish Clancy, Sean Cummins, Angela Dressel, David Emerson, Pamela Fairnington, Tim Gill, Jack Handley, Greg Harper, Elizabeth Hooley, Penny Jensz, Anna Johnson, Carole-Anne Lang, Nigel Lang, Sheila Lang, Sidney Lang, Frances Lefroy, Jamie MacFadyen, David Mackrell, Christina Martin, Andrew Masterson, Verica Meric, Corey Mitchell, Scott Murray, Roger Nance, Christine Parris, Matthew Quick, Robert Quick, Jeevan Rajah, Sally Rajah, Vivi Rajah, Sawthirajah Ramalingam, Leanne Rogers, Karen Schooling, Craig Scrivener, John Skaro, Julian Smith, Trevor Smith, Mark Sofilas, Jane Staples, Alissa Tanskya, Philippa Vanderguten and Sharyn Wortman.

Extra special thanks to Andrew Wilson and Jim Everard of

Wilson Everard Advertising for their support and encouragement, particularly during office hours when we were meant to be writing ads, not dreaming up books.

Last but not least, thanks to the following – without whom this book could very well not have been possible: Aaron, Aiden, Alan, Andrew, Andy, Brett, Cameron, Craig, Darren, Don, Frank, Geoffrey, Grant, Greg, Jeff, Jim, James, Jimmy, John, Martin, Mark, Matthew, Michael, Mike, Nigel, Paul, Richard, Robert, Rodney, Simon, Shane, Tim, Tony, William and Zebedee.

Discontents

We-Love-You-We-Love-You-Not
AIR SIGNS

Don't-Hate-Us-'Cos-We're-Wishy-Washy
WATER SIGNS

Which BASTARD for which GODDESS?

Forewarned

This is not one of those ever-so-nice, tiresomely tactful zodiac guides. You know the sort: 'His axe-murdering tendencies are more than made up for by his buckets of charm.' If you're looking for signs of hope, go read a real astrology book.

How to Spot a B*st*rd by his Star Sign is a no-nonsense, warts-and-all exposé on men and how their star signs bring out the bastards in all of them. In other words, it's just a bloody good excuse to slag off every guy we've ever loved and lost – without being slapped with legal writs.

We don't profess to be real astrologers. We don't have to adopt silly names and wear kaftans to be able to pigeonhole a man by his date of birth. We just have to date him.

Needless to say, both of us have an extensive working knowledge of the subject (that is, we're total trollops who have bonked busloads of bastards). And even if our research isn't completely astrologically sound, it does make for a rollicking good read.

So, when you think you've met the man of your dreams, dip into this garrulous guide and find his flaws before you make a lunge. That way you won't have anyone to blame but yourself when he turns out to be a scuzzbag-from-hell.

If you're reading *How to Spot a B*st*rd by his Star Sign* to bone up on a current lover, you're probably in too deep to leave him well enough alone. But at least using our malicious musings you can constantly point out his failings to him and break his spirit as quickly as possible.

Of course, if you've just come out of a traumatic twosome you can pounce on all our put-downs and gain some small comfort from knowing your ex-other-half really *was* a born loser.

It's up to you. You can rely on *How to Spot a B*st*rd by his Star Sign* to bring your girlish hopes and dreams down to earth with a resounding thud. Or you can regard it as the rantings of two embittered and twisted man-haters – which you will if you fancy some bloke like mad. Just don't say we didn't warn you.

Adèle Lang and Susi Rajah

PS to any man who accidentally-on-purpose picks up this book. It was written about you, not for you. You won't agree with any of it. Especially if you're Aries, Taurus, Gemini, Cancer, Leo, Virgo, Libra, Scorpio, Sagittarius, Capricorn, Aquarius or Pisces. However, if you do have a bit of a self-deprecating chuckle, then you're probably not a bastard after all. You probably also live on another planet and have never dated a woman in your entire life.

We're-Hot-So-Shut-Up-And-Worship-Us

FIRE SIGNS

Aries, Leo, Sagittarius

Out-of-control control-freaks. Untalented show-offs. Pig-ignorant know-it-alls. And that's their good points. These self-proclaimed demi-gods will try to get your attention at the merest hint of provocation (e.g. you happen to be in the same room as them).

Fire Sign Bastards are always better than you and will never fail to tell you so. They'll then hammer the fact home by telling you again – just in case you didn't hear them the first time.

Dare to disagree and they'll act in their usual endearing way. They'll start yelling, turn puce and then hurl themselves to the ground with much thrashing about of arms and legs. Five minutes later they'll get back up again and act as if nothing's happened. Real astrologers like to call this their 'quick temperedness'. We like to call men in white coats.

Of course, you could choose to ignore Fire Sign Bastards and hope they'll just go away. Like, right. Why go off and voluntarily die when they can be humoured one-thousand-four-hundred and forty-four minutes a day?

However, if the thought of kneeling at their feet in mock-wonder does make you want to throw up, don't worry. You won't have to do it for long. Fire Sign Bastards are such temperamental, competitive sons of bastards, they usually die early of heart attacks.

The Aries Bastard

21 MARCH–20 APRIL

Once upon a time, in the dark ages, there was this quaint little term known as a *man's man*. Nobody quite knew what it meant. Except the poor unfortunate thing who was the *man's man's woman* – and she died a horrible death when she wilfully stuck her head in the oven unto which she was chained.

Then comes the enlightened nineties and in minces the sensitive New Age Feeling Fellow. All of a sudden, a man's man surely must mean a gentleman of the pink persuasion and, gee, don't those scented candles look too, too, utterly, utterly?

Meanwhile, back at the camp, deep in the woods, a solitary male is yelling at the top of his lungs, beating a tom-tom and sticking pins into a blow-up doll that looks a lot like Germaine

Greer. This sad, lost soul is the Aries bloke. Bewildered by beauty myths, dumbfounded by daycare centres and completely baffled by consensual sex, he holds on to his masculinity as tightly as he holds on to his manhood (which is throbbing if you must know). Boy, does he yearn for the times when men were men and women were grateful.

Being the only *man's man* left in existence, it's lonely for him at the bottom of the food chain – even the amoeba, given the chance, opt to mate with themselves.

And thank bloody Christ for that. Aries is such a chauvinist he'd root for truffles if he knew what truffles actually were. He's exactly the type of guy who thinks any man who buys scented candles is a raving poofter.

So, if the bastard you fancy puts on Vivaldi in the evening, whips up a nice little *soufflé a deux* and then settles down to read Jane Austen to you, he's almost certainly gay and he's definitely not Aries. Because even an Aries fairy would be down the local hellfire club, dressed to the cat-o'-nines and slugging back Frangelico with his like-minded friends.

All Aries men enjoy hanging out at the pub with their mates. And even the dead-straight homophobic one doesn't think twice about getting sentimental with them when he's pissed. In fact, you'll swear he must be an open-and-shut closet case since he spends far more time hugging and kissing other blokes than he ever does you.

The real reason this revolting creature prefers the company of men is because he has no choice. No right-thinking woman with two opposable thumbs and lack of tail can bear the thought of being in the same room at the same time as him. He exudes so much testosterone that not only will the fine hairs on the nape of her neck stand up, they'll actually go through a rapid growth spurt.

If you are unfortunate enough to be stuck in an enclosed space with Aries, it's best just to smile as vacuously as you can and nod your head at appropriate intervals – because you won't understand a single word he's saying. English is his second language, grunting is his first. And all he can grunt about is himself, his career, his sporting achievements and how feminists would be a lot less upright if he gave them all a good shag.

Of course, *good* and *shag* are polar opposites when it comes to this rock-throwing Romeo. One night with Aries is enough to get thee, Linda Lovelace, to the nunnery. To put it as delicately as we can, let's just say that you won't actually have time to lie back and think of England.

Despite his obvious lack of sexual stamina, the Aries bastard feels biologically compelled to pursue any number of luckless ladies with a vengeance verging on primeval. His courting tactics are as subtle as a sledgehammer and not half as useful. So for God's sake don't play hard to get. It'll only encourage him.

He'll use gorilla tactics to win you over. And why shouldn't you be flattered to be woken at three in the morning to see his great hairy face leering through your fifth-floor bedroom window? Especially when you're entertaining a guest who just so happens to be male, totally hetero and sensitive to boot.

Said guest is likely to be kicked by said boot out of aforementioned window (which is closed). Walls will be perforated, furniture dismantled and sincere apologies extracted from you who are, by now, a sobbing heap in the corner putting the women's movement back centuries.

As he's just proven, and which he'll take great pains to point ,
out he's not in the least bit jealous or possessive. It's just that he
likes the idea of loyalty and faithfulness. From you, that is. He'll
stay faithful for as long as you stay perfect. Which you're not.
Which he'll tell you, ad nauseam. (*Little known fact here: not only
is the Aries bastard God's gift to women, he actually is God. And we
all know what happens to those who don't believe in God. However,
a few years with Aries and hell will suddenly seem like a really
inviting option.*) If you want to know your hair is a mess, you can't
drive your car for shit and you could do with a self-help course,
then you can't go wrong with Aries.

Funnily enough, it's not the same the other way round. This
hypocritical oaf is quite capable of pointing out your dimply
thighs without giving so much as a thought to his own
disgusting flab. Don't bother picking him up on this though –
the subtleties of irony will be lost in translation.

So, if you like being told what to do, how to do it and when
to do it, this one's for you. If you have a mind of your own and
occasionally like to use it, tell him to get lost. But put the kettle
on and warm his slippers before you go.

If you decide to leave, don't expect him to take it lying down.
Lying down is your job. In the game of life, the term 'gracious
in defeat' is hard enough for Aries to pronounce, let alone
practise. Beat him at something as trivial as Scrabble and he'll
proclaim – once he's started speaking to you again – that
Scrabble is a game of luck, requires absolutely no intelligence
and besides, you got all the A's, B's and C's and he got all the Q's,
X's and Z's and no vowels whatsoever.

Of course, no matter which way you play it you can't win.
Because he's even more unbearable on the extremely rare

occasion he does manage to outwit you. He'll crow that Scrabble is a game of skill and bang on about how he managed to make really big words like CAT out of very hard letters like Q, X and Z. (*Note: If he does attempt to be humble in victory, he's just fishing for compliments. Don't give him any.*)

Since Aries can't cope with you beating him at a board game, it therefore follows he'll be positively suicidal if you outdo him in the boardroom. So quit before you get ahead. Because if you do start scoring more fame, fortune and frequent flier points than him, he'll just try and get you pregnant.

HOW TO SPOT ONE
Throw peanuts. If he catches them in his mouth, he's probably Aries. But if he then starts beating his chest and picking lint off your clothes, he's definitely Aries. This means he will have a big fat (red and ugly) behind. This is to balance his big fat 'ditto' head.

WHERE TO FIND ONE
Commandeering a cave. Moving his lips whilst reading *The Cat in the Hat*. Or marching at a Real Men Against Women's Rights To Answer Back rally. If he's in the kitchen, he's obviously lost.

HOW TO INTRIGUE ONE
This is tricky because you need to be two things at once. You've got to be loud and obnoxious so he thinks he's found his soul mate. At the same time you must show your soft, feminine side so his masculinity isn't threatened. The best way to do both simultaneously is to hurl spitballs at the pavement whilst taking care not to hit your Laura Ashley frock.

THE FIRST DATE
He'll either take you to the zoo to meet his family or else he'll invite you to the annual Especially Privileged Ladies' Night at the Masonic Lodge and tell you what you'd like to eat, how much you'd like to drink and be horrified when you attempt to open your mouth for anything other than eating, drinking and sucking.

WHEN TO DO THE DEED
Whenever. If he doesn't have honourable intentions, he'll think you're a slut but have sex with you anyway. If he does like you, he'll still have sex with you and then wake you up to propose.

WHEN TO POP THE QUESTION
Don't. That's a man's job. Just relax and enjoy your independence whilst you still have it. You'll have years to regret giving it up.

IF HE DROPS YOU
Forget him. Since the Aries bastard is incapable of admitting he's wrong – particularly in front of a woman – he's hardly likely to come loping back into your life declaring it was all a big mistake. If he does, it's only because no other woman will have him.

IF YOU DROP HIM
He'll chase you because it won't occur to him that you can ignore his sheer animal magnetism. Keep running. He'll trip over his knuckles sooner or later.

The Leo Bastard

24 July–23 August

Introductory note: It must be pointed out Mr Leo's play is yet to be performed in a real theatre. But we are informed by Mr Leo this is due to protracted negotiations with producers in London who are terribly anxious to buy the rights. Indeed – as Mr Leo himself said – this play has 'West End' written all over it. And even taking into account this is the first play Mr Leo has penned – in fact his first piece of creative writing since high school – we have to say (*because he is forcing us to*) he is an outstanding master of the genre. This is a model modern short play. It displays an art of construction one usually only expects from the most revered and respected of writers. (Is that enough?) His dialogue, too, is worthy of much praise. Its deftness defies description; it never halts; it moves from beginning to end without a dull moment. And it's so amazingly true to life. Except wittier. And sharper. And more poignant. Its sheer brilliance will astound you and leave you gasping for more. (*There, satisfied now?*) We truly appreciate Mr Leo's generosity in allowing us to print his amazing, soon-to-be-much-lauded play in this most unworthy tome.

THE LOVES OF LEO

Written by Leo. Produced by Leo. Directed by Leo. Starring Leo.

Important: No performance of this play may be given unless written permission has been obtained from Leo and he is allowed to produce, direct and star in it.

CAST OF CHARACTERS
Leo, played by himself. (*The unbelievably dashing, irresistible, courageous – not to mention terrifically handsome – hero of the play, around whom all action revolves.*)

The Beautiful** Heroine, played by you. (*Minor though important supporting role.*)

The Beautiful**-Heroine's More-Beautiful**Rival, in this instance played by Uma Thurman. (*This is the role every other woman on earth is vying for. The purpose of this character is to make the heroine realise just what she is up against and to make her suitably grateful when Leo finally chooses her.*)

The Much-Less-Exciting Man, played by someone like Daniel Day-Lewis or Brad Pitt. (*This role is really just that of an extra – a clever plot device to point out how inferior all other men are to Leo. Naturally, there is no chance of the heroine or any other woman in the world preferring this lesser man to Leo.*)

The Beautiful** Maid, played by you. (*Again, another minor though important supporting role.*)

Leo had initially wanted to write *The Loves of Leo: A Midsummer Night's Dream* but someone named William-something had thoughtlessly used the title first. It goes without saying, Leo's

23

version would have been much better.

** Though not as beautiful as Leo.

The Very Appreciative Audience, played by you, Uma Thurman and all the other men in the world.

NB: All the characters are in modern costume. Leo is wearing faultless, immaculately tailored evening clothes which set off his hair, height and colouring perfectly. As for the rest of the cast, well, it doesn't really matter what they're wearing, does it?

ACT ONE

Scene: The tastefully and delightfully appointed drawing-room of Leo's house. The Beautiful Heroine, The Beautiful-Heroine's-More-Beautiful Rival and The Much-Less-Exciting Man are all present and seated. [*The Very Appreciative Audience is also present but not visible.*] There is an air of melancholy about the three as they are all desperately missing the sparkling presence of their charming host who has momentarily left the room. After a couple of suspense-filled minutes, the drawing-room doors are flung open with a flourish and Leo enters, causing the whole room to look brighter as a result of his charming sparkling presence.

Leo [*looking around*]: Hello, everybody. Why so glum? Have you been missing the sparkling presence of your charming host?
   [*The Very Appreciative Audience bursts into wild applause making it impossible for the play to continue for about five minutes.*]

Leo [*starting to speak amid the subsiding applause, longing sighs and occasional fainting of The Very Appreciative Audience – showing all the world he is not the egotist he is wrongfully reported to be*]: Well? [*Once again, Leo shows why he is regarded as the saviour of the lost art of drawing-room conversation.*]

The Beautiful Heroine and the Beautiful-Heroine's-More-Beautiful Rival [*in unison whilst gazing adoringly at Leo – as one does*]: Yes, we missed you terribly. Life is not the same without you.

Leo [*brushing off this blatant but understandable adoration*]: How about a drink, then? Where is that maid of mine? [*spotting The Beautiful Heroine*] Get us all a drink will you, love?

[*The Beautiful Heroine/Maid scurries off to do as she has been asked, grateful to be of use to her – and everybody's – hero.*]

The Much-Less-Exciting Man [*opens his mouth to say something*]: Um . . . [*He realises just in time he can never say anything to compare to the witty, intelligent conversation of Leo and politely leaves the room in recognition of the other man's natural superiority.*]

Leo: Rather flighty chap, isn't he? [*allowing us a glimpse of the true understanding of human nature present in this exceptional man. Indeed, it causes much murmuring in The Very Appreciative Audience. At this point The Beautiful Heroine returns to the room with drinks for everyone. Neither she nor The Beautiful-Heroine's-More-Beautiful Rival even notices The Much-Less-Exciting Man has left. It is difficult for them to notice anyone else when Leo is in the room.*]

Leo [*taking a drink and a handful of the delicate, mouth-watering pastries The Beautiful Heroine whipped up whilst she was fetching the drinks*]: Hey, these are good.

How to Spot a B*st*rd by his Star Sign

[*The Very Appreciative Audience spontaneously bursts into thunderous cheering at this heartfelt compliment to The Beautiful Heroine because it indicates Leo knows women like it when you say nice stuff to them and also shows he is not swayed by mere physical beauty. After all, The Beautiful-Heroine's-More-Beautiful Rival is better looking but Leo never said anything to her.*]

Leo [*playing to the audience*]: Yes [*nods, causing himself to look even more thoughtful and handsome*]. Very good, indeed. [*The Very Appreciative Audience erupts once more and The Beautiful-Heroine's-More-Beautiful Rival dashes off to the kitchen in an attempt to gain Leo's attention.*]

Leo [*to The Beautiful Heroine, demonstrating his awesome powers of observation*]: It looks like we're alone.

CURTAIN

[*The Very Appreciative Audience leaps to its collective feet to give a two-hour standing ovation to the genius responsible for the play.*]

Concluding note: Once again, Mr Leo has requested we point out the brilliance of his play, this time by focusing on the gargantuan intellect it must have taken to produce the cliffhanger ending. Naturally, he won't leave you in suspense forever and we're sure you'll all await the sequel with bated breath. He's going to call it *The Loves of Leo II: To Be Or Not To Be*. Okay, look, you tell him it's been done before. We've had it.

HOW TO SPOT ONE
His entrance will always be preceded by a drum-roll. If you miss his entrance you'll find him already strategically positioned

under a spotlight. You can't miss him there – not with the two game show hostesses on either side of him pointing him out. You might also notice The Hand of God above his head scrawling a cloudy message in the air: Women of the world, my gift to you. Regards, God. PS: Those of you who don't believe in Me can also have him.

WHERE TO FIND ONE
Anywhere there is an audience of at least one.

HOW TO INTRIGUE ONE
Look up at him in wonder and say ingeniously: 'My, what a big, strong man you are', 'Gee, I wish I was as smart/witty/brave as you' or 'Are you a famous movie star?' Or just wear a full-length mirror around your neck and don't say anything at all.

THE FIRST DATE
The first date will be quite enjoyable. You won't have ever heard all his stories about himself so you'll find them quite entertaining. They're even bearable when you hear them for the second time on your second date.

WHEN TO DO THE DEED
On the third date. You need to do something to avoid hearing his life story again and sex will shut him up nicely. Of course, earplugs or refusing to see him any more would have the same effect but we're working under the assumption he is – that, in the course of two dates, you will have fallen madly in love with him and now find it impossible to live without him.

How to Spot a B*st*rd by his Star Sign

WHEN TO POP THE QUESTION

He'll decide when you want to get married. Just be ready to answer with a breathless 'Yes, of course' when he lets you know where and when the wedding's taking place. Then pretend your tears are caused by joy when he shows you the lace monstrosity you'll be wearing. And appear to be suitably grateful when he informs you you're allowed to choose one bridesmaid to go with the six he's already selected.

IF HE DROPS YOU

Did you dare to leave your much-sought-after position at his feet being adoring in order to go to work? Did you exchange entire sentences with another man (never mind that he was your brother-in-law)? Did you have a point of view other than his? Or did you laugh at him when he wasn't being intentionally funny? Well, then, we're not surprised. You had it coming to you.

IF YOU DROP HIM

That you'd want to do this is completely beyond the realms of possibility.

The Sagittarius Bastard

23 NOVEMBER–21 DECEMBER

PS: Sagittarius does everything back to front. He speaks before he thinks, leaps before he looks and loves you only after you've left him. Which is why when people say Sagittarius is a lucky bastard, they're dead right. The fact that you haven't murdered him yet is a miracle. The fact that his other girlfriends haven't either is a godsend. The fact that real astrologers can find pleasant things to say about him, wasting entire virgin rainforests in the process, is pure magic.

In the olden days, philosophers used to comfort themselves with the knowledge that: 'I think, therefore I am not Sagittarius.' No small thanks to me and a proliferation of Piscean protest groups who didn't like victimisation of any kind unless it was specifically directed at them, the phrase became bastardised somewhat and now Sagittarius still wouldn't have a clue what it meant.

What the wise old men of yore were trying to say, no doubt, is that the Sagittarius bastard dives head-first into mind-bogglingly unsuitable situations without so much as a second thought because first ones are hard enough.

Then, when what men and women of science kindly refer to as his 'brain' has had time to catch up with his actions, he jumps back out again just as quickly. (In a perfect world, men who acted on impulse would send flowers to teenage girls who used cheap deodorant and leave it at that. This, however, is the real world, and in the real world you've got Sagittarius running amok getting teenage girls pregnant and then leaving them for even younger girls who wear even cheaper deodorant.)

More irritating than the cold sores you'll mysteriously begin to develop, is the fact that Sagittarius is the one who started it all in the first place by hurling himself at your feet, literally begging to be enslaved. But as soon as you experience that warm fuzzy feeling in the pit of your stomach commonly known as love/ulcer/morning sickness, he's up and off.

It's not because you aren't the love of his life – don't get him wrong. It's just that now he's had time to think (*sic*) about it, he's finally realised current relationship problems could be due to the fact you're a black, radical feminist-communist whose favourite pastime is abseiling and he's a white, moderate chauvinist-fascist who's terrified of scaling great heights.

The Sagittarius bastard's blind refusal to contemplate foresight before hindsight could be excused (because by now you'll have realised what you aren't missing) if at the same time he didn't have the temerity to tell you it was all your fault and that you tricked him into it.

You didn't *tell* him you were black. And why *shouldn't* he think the extremely rare and valuable lithograph of Joseph Stalin above your mantelpiece was a portrait of your dad? And how was he to know you were a die-hard feminist? You cooked dinner for him once, *didn't* you? Okay, yes, he did have to pick your underarm hair out of the pasta, but so?

Frankly, it just serves as a good excuse for him to be as unfaithful as he likes without all the boring guilt that goes along with it.

To say Sagittarius has a deep-rooted fear of monogamy is to say Salman Rushdie is slightly perturbed about dying. Indeed, advertising wankers have been able to retire on the government proceeds they received for the rash of safe sex campaigns created especially for all the Sagittarius bastards' girlfriends. (The original slogan: 'Avoid Sagittarius like the plague, otherwise you'll end up catching it' was ditched during research when the male Scorpio component complained about out-and-out favouritism.)

Sagittarius doesn't own a stereo, not because he can't afford one (which he can't) but because the word hi-fidelity sends him into a cold sweat as opposed to the hot one he got after the last dose of hepatitis.

Truth be said though, the Sagittarius bastard's honesty is something to behold. If he's screwed around he'll tell you. In excruciating detail. When you gently hint you don't care to know who put his hand where, he'll put his great big foot in his great big mouth and tell you that, well, actually, come to think about it, it wasn't actually a hand, it was . . . (at this stage you are fully within your rights to put your hand, which is clenched, into his mouth, which is open, and fill it full of loose teeth).

If and when you meet his family, you'll notice they too are hideously embarrassed by his tactless words and thoughtless manner. You'll soon appreciate why he was kicked out of home at an early age and is only ever allowed back for major family get-togethers. Like funerals. And even then, in others' darkest hours, he still can't help but dig himself into a very large hole.

Asking his sister where her husband is (he's the one in the coffin) is a good example of one of his more minor gaffes. In a hurried attempt to make amends, he'll tell her he was only joking. When she promptly bursts into tears, he'll try and make her feel better by saying he didn't think she and her now-dead spouse were all that well suited anyway.

If the monumental blunders weren't bad enough, there's always the obligatory Sagittarius bluster to make you wish the ground would open up and swallow him. Since he doesn't have two IQ points to rub together, Sagittarius doesn't actually realise he's an intellectual dwarf. So, at the wake, this walking clap-trap will regale you and his relatives with facts about which he knows absolutely nothing – completely oblivious to the fact the lot of you are pointedly snoring. Ancient embalming techniques, Celtic burial rites and the psychological effects of reincarnation upon loopy Hollywood actresses, you name it, Sagittarius will be able to prattle on without a pause.

Take him to task about his source and he'll say he read it in a book. Since you know he doesn't read anything he hasn't written himself and you just *know* he can't write because you do his remedial English assignments for him, you'll feel compelled to point out to him that *Playboy* doesn't count. Any rare pearls of wisdom which do accidentally stream from his lips are usually poached from someone who's more intellectually gifted. Like you, for example.

Which brings us to our next point. If you're so smart, what the hell are you doing dating him? And don't start telling us it's because he's *generous*.

Yes, Sagittarius might scatter money around as profligately as his seed. But this isn't generosity, this is fiscal promiscuity. Once he's spent all his money and his family's money, he'll start spending yours. When that runs out he'll proceed to spend the earnings of his other girlfriends. Then the bank's. Then the credit union's. And then the loan shark's.

Again it won't be his fault when he's eventually had up for bankruptcy/embezzlement/fraud in a supreme court or else found in some squalid bedsit sharing pillows with a horse's head. Why didn't you *tell* him those things with all the columns of numbers were loan default statements? How was *he* to know the anonymous letters featuring clipped-out-of-the-newspaper words like PAY, UP, OR, YOU and DIE were death threats? Anyway, what are *you* doing still hanging around? Didn't he *leave* you? And don't say you're still with him because he's a bloody lucky bastard. He *knows* that. What d'you think he is? *Stupid?*

HOW TO SPOT ONE
He's usually long of limb and short of cash. The wandering eye is not an optical dysfunction, no matter how many times he tries to convince you otherwise.

WHERE TO FIND ONE
In a flotation tank clearing his head. In a think tank feeling out of his depth. At a bank asking for credit. At a brothel making a deposit.

HOW TO INTRIGUE ONE
Act intelligent.

THE FIRST DATE
If he thinks he can get you into bed, expect to be lavished. Just don't be surprised when the debt collectors arrive at the restaurant to take away your meal.

WHEN TO DO THE DEED
Do so at your own risk. If you start developing facial lesions and can't shake that particularly nasty bout of pneumonia, seek medical advice immediately.

How to Spot a B*st*rd by his Star Sign

WHEN TO POP THE QUESTION
When you decide you'd like to be a divorcee in the not-too-distant future.

IF HE DROPS YOU
Count yourself lucky but feign devastation nonetheless. And make sure he pays you the money he owes you.

IF YOU DROP HIM
It'll take some time for the words to sink in. So start day one with 'You're', day two with 'dropped' and on day three really put the knife in with 'thicko'.

Hi-We're-The-Most-Boring-Men-On

EARTH SIGNS

Taurus, Virgo, Capricorn

'Safe, solid and reliable' can be used to describe a very large bank. Or a bloody boring man.

Earth Sign Bastards are the astrological nice guys. That's not a horrible thing to say? Okay, recall the last time a man was bowled over when you told him he was 'a really nice guy but . . .'? Who wants to date someone only your mother could love?

Of course, she'll adore the fact your Earth Sign Bastard boyfriends can remember the birthdays of all her grandchildren and can name every single one of the 40,000 varieties of flora and fauna in her backyard – *in Latin*.

Your dad will be similarly impressed by your Earth Sign Bastard boyfriends' ability to fill in tax forms properly, as well as their distinct inability to have dishonourable attentions towards his daughter.

Seriously though, if you do want to wear unflattering white for a day, experience agonising labour pains and take on a crippling mortgage, then snag one of these bastards. They're so determined to do everything by rote, marriage with them really will appear to last for ever and ever.

Because they never take exciting risks or indulge in fun-fun-fun vices, Earth Sign Bastards live long and healthy lives. With a bit of luck though, they'll bore you to death. Preferably sooner rather than later.

The Taurus Bastard

21 April–21 May

You're weaning yourself off the lithium and you're in the process of finding a new job, savings account and country to live in. In other words, you're in the delicate process of recovering from a horrendous relationship with a total bastard (Aries, Scorpio and Pisces spring to mind here, for no apparent reason).

Who better than Taurus to charge into your life and help put you on the straight and narrow? The one man in the universe who seriously knows what's good for you and goes about giving it to you, no matter how many times you tell him to sod off . . . At this point we could cut an interminably long rant short by saying Hitler was a Taurus. But we can't as the small army of the bloody bastards breathing down our necks won't let us . . . Therefore, while you look helplessly on, Taurus will storm up and down the war office that's masquerading as a lounge-room, issuing arrest warrants, editorial comments and rent tribunal complaints on your behalf.

If you so much as *attempt* to get up to make yourself another glass of his fortifying home brew, he'll bark at you to sit back down again as you don't need to stand on your own two feet whilst he's around. This usually has the effect of making you feel a bit redundant and fools him into dangerously misguided beliefs like he's being incredibly useful. Don't think you're being unreasonable if, after a while, you feel like you don't have a thought of your own. Even if you did, Taurus wouldn't agree.

For argument's sake, let's say that whilst gulping down the twelfth dodgy beer he brought, you chance upon the Virgin Mary glowering virtuously above the drinks cabinet. After you excitedly tell him about your immaculate discovery, he'll declare there's no such thing as God and you must be on drugs (which is not far from the truth since you've doubled your lithium intake in the vague hope you'll accidentally overdose).

However, you still have some of your faculties intact; one of which is pride. But even when you cross yourself, stand tall and point to Our Mary, Mother of God, whilst waving your diploma in Astrophysics, your degree in Visual Arts and your Masters in Biblical Communications under his nose, he'll still insist you don't know what you're talking about. As far as Taurus is concerned, you're completely incapable of saying or doing anything by yourself. That's where he comes in. Again.

You casually mention that now you've got your PhD in Social Sciences and once you can face people again, you think it might be quite nice to have a career. Before you know it, there's a party plan rep making nuisance calls. (Taurus is a tad old-fashioned that way. Career girls aren't his cup of tea unless they actually make it for a living.)

You mention in passing that once you've got over your fear of wide-open spaces, you'd quite like a holiday sometime in the near distant future. Done. Booked. Paid for. Where? Why do you need to know? What's wrong with Poland? You'll like it. They don't eat either.

You then let slip that, one day, when you're well enough, you might like to have a baby. Lo and behold, he waltzes into the bedroom waggling a thermometer, plotting your biorhythms and methodically filling in the appropriate forms to ensure young Taurus isn't left on the waiting list for Scouts.

The Taurus bastard is so big on practicalities that before too long he'll be making your toes curl which the doctors say is an encouraging sign since they had resigned themselves to you being a complete vegetable for the rest of your life.

You wouldn't mind so much if he came up with solutions in a less predictably earnest and efficient manner. Then at least there'd be a bit of gratuitous excitement, a spot of feckless recklessness to enjoy from the comfort of your coma. But to put it as politely as possible, Taurus is one of life's plodders. And whilst slow and steady may win the master race, it's pretty goddamn tortuous to watch or to participate in (which is probably why you're still on the lithium and have quietly developed a methadone habit as well).

Paradoxically, when he's not running and therefore ruining your life for you, the Taurus bastard is busy being chronically lazy. When it comes to doing things for himself he won't move unless he has to (i.e. to the fridge, the fridge or the bar-fridge). If he lives by himself, don't be ecstatic when he invites you over to his place. It'll look like a bomb's hit it and this may very well be the case if he still lives in that bunker in Berlin.

His sloth-like ways do not bode well for what we will *generously* describe as your 'sex life' with him. Though Taurus likes to be in control when upright, he'll always allow you to be on top in bed. Indeed, he's so bone idle the only kind of rapid eye movement you're ever likely to experience is when you're fast asleep.

Propaganda issued from the Earth Sign Camp decrees that, yes, he can be a bit of a couch potato but he is indescribably loyal, so yah boo sucks. Since when loyalty has been such a hallowed virtue is completely beyond our realms of comprehension. That rare breed of man who is faithful usually expects it to be returned in spades. If you, understandably, like the odd bit of extra-curricular nookie just for variety, forget it. Another guy so much as looks at you and he'll be dead where he stands.

As for you, well, Taurus won't tick you off immediately. He'll just keep your innumerable betrayals on his mental scoreboard. Then, when your quota's up, he'll dismiss you. Ruthlessly. This can get a bit confusing because the last straw could be the fact you didn't pick up the groceries on your way home (you've finally been allowed out on your own, as long as it's only to the corner shop). So you'll go through life believing Taurus dropped you because you forgot the milk not because you were having it off with his best friend.

And whilst you can plead your case until the cows come home, once he's made up his mind about something, *nothing* will force him to reconsider. Threats involving kitchen appliances or power tools don't work unless a prison sentence for manslaughter seems preferable to putting up with his pigheadedness. Be warned though. If you *do* attempt to kill him and you aren't completely successful, he'll hold it against you for the rest of your life. When Taurus has a gripe about something, you will never, *ever* hear the end of it. On and on and on he'll go – he got rejected from art college, his mother didn't love him, his German Shepherd got run over (*repeat as often as you like for maximum desired effect*).

Our only advice here is to make the most of your rapidly deteriorating mental health by raving like a maniac. That means he'll be forced to stop doing likewise and be helpful for once by rushing round trying to find you a good psychiatrist.

HOW TO SPOT ONE
The odd-shaped skull, slightly bovine features and pot belly are usually dead giveaways. However, if he's also got a moustache, a forelock and a syphilitic nose, call Mossed immediately.

WHERE TO FIND ONE
Standing over you, lying under you or sitting in a seat on behalf of a completely daft political party. If by fat chance he's running anywhere it'll be on doctor's orders.

HOW TO INTRIGUE ONE
Look as unfetching as you can in your wheelchair. When he smiles at you, turn a blind eye and stare pointedly at the golden Labrador seated next to you. When he doesn't get the

hint and instead says, '*Guten morgen*', pretend to be deaf and use sign language to make him go away. When he still refuses to take 'fuck off' for an answer and persists in asking you out, pretend you're also mute so you don't have to say 'yes'.

THE FIRST DATE
He'll push you kicking and screaming in your wheelchair to a beer festival. There he'll devour all the bratwurst and sauerkraut within gobbling range whilst you drink the lager tent dry in a dismal attempt to forget.

WHEN TO DO THE DEED
Join the resistance and don't.

WHEN TO POP THE QUESTION
When you're fed up with all the vicarious thrills and tumultuous times provided by less dependable but ultimately more desirable bastards. And only after you've quit your drug problem and practised your goosestep so you can walk down the aisle in a straight line.

IF HE DROPS YOU
He won't. Tenacity is his only virtue. Drop him instead.

IF YOU DROP HIM
He'll patiently wait for you to realise your disastrous mistake. When you don't, he'll patiently wait until you do.

The Virgo Bastard

24 August–23 September

Ever wondered what goes on in the mind of a serial killer? Find out what Interpol has been trying to discover for years and date a Virgo bastard. Because, if you're going to be a successful psychopath, you have to:

- enjoy repeating the same tedious task in the same mind-numbing fashion
- have an unhealthy obsession with the little details – details normal people can't be bothered with because they've got lives
- be too thick-skinned to notice people crossing to the opposite side of the street when they see you
- write checklists to ensure you do everything you keep threatening to do.

If you're currently in love with Virgo and you don't want to believe the truth ('he seems such a nice, quiet, unassuming kind of guy'), pick up any detective novel that features an icepick-wielding nutter and then try telling us he doesn't remind you of someone you know and it's all just a bunch of alarming coincidences.

Let's face it, massive generalisations and sweeping statements aside, the circumstantial evidence is overwhelming. Like the odd little habits Serial Killer-slash-Virgo picked up in childhood. Even if you replace pulling wings off insects with stamp collecting, exchange bed-wetting for train-spotting and substitute a fascination with lighting fires for an unhealthy interest in algebra, you've got to admit the similarities are pretty disturbing.

This budding Bates is so spine-tinglingly awful, his own mother encourages him to take lollies off strangers and tries to lose him in shopping centres. If she's lucky – and he takes her advice about only crossing roads when the red man is flashing – she won't have to put up with him telling her how to defrost her fridge correctly.

Then there's the usual (yawn) teenage angst that turns the slightly creepy, pale, skinny youth into a veritable walking time-bomb. A traumatic experience like the fact people make it patently obvious they hate his guts because he's so bloody anal is usually a good place to start. His well-scrubbed, clean-cut features and neatly creased trousers make it only right that other boys should want to beat him up. The fact he can't understand why they pick on him gives them all the more reason to do so.

And who can blame the girls for refusing to kiss him behind the school lavatory? To do so means he'd be close enough to scrutinise them. Serial Killer-slash-Virgo is such a nit-picker he won't just see the spots on their chins, he'll also see the blackheads, whiteheads, open pores and broken capillaries. And if he does happen to be staring deeply into their eyes, it's a dead cert he's moonlighting as an iridologist.

No wonder the adult version is so unsuccessful with women (which, by the way, is another tired excuse the average psycho uses to justify his anti-social behaviour when the overweight, chain-smoking alcoholic/detective eventually catches up with him). That penetrating Virgo gaze will turn you into a quivering mass of neuroses in no time. Yes, you could choose to do it with the lights off, but then you wouldn't be able to see him reach under the bed for his icepick.

It goes without saying he'll also put your domestic habits under the microscope. If you're the kind of girl who thinks housework means waving a vacuum cleaner in the general vicinity of the living-room, you're going to drive Virgo insane (which takes quite a lot of doing since 'drive' and 'Virgo' don't exactly go hand in hand). Likewise, if your idea of cleaning the bathtub consists of chucking in a bar of soap whilst douching, prepare for problems.

Of course, we're not for one moment suggesting you'll end up on his things-to-do list. And look on the bright side anyway: ending up dead will be a lot less painful in the long run than putting up with his incessant nagging. Virgo's obsession with *your* domestic hygiene borders on the pathological. The reason for this is obvious to everyone save fat detectives stalking serial killers.

Leave him to his own devices and he's wont to sit quite happily in his own mess for months at a time. However, if *you* keep his house sparkling clean, the people from forensic aren't going to be able to pick up the stray hair, blood and bone off the living-room carpet.

Having said all this, there is one vice authors habitually omit when describing Virgo's less endearing qualities. And that's because even they are too appalled to bring themselves to put it down on paper. Whippings and beatings they can happily handle. Lashings of liver and buckets of blood they can just about stomach. But let's not talk about [insert stage-managed whisper here] *his spending habits.*

It would be a gross miscarriage of justice to call Virgo mean with money. 'Mean' is an inoffensive little word that cannot hope to conjure up the penurious ways of this bastard. Instead, try calling him 'an outrageous tightwad who would steal the coins out of a blind man's hat if he thought no one was looking'.

Virgo is so careful with his cash, he never actually leaves home *with* it. However, he's quite willing to let you spend yours – usually on expensive suits for him to replace the bloodstained ones he'd had to put in at the drycleaners.

As with all his other bad behaviour, there is a deep-rooted psychological excuse for his skinflint shenanigans: since his clients don't pay him for the work he does on their behalf, nor do they leave him anything in their wills, he's bound to be financially bereft.

Indeed, to cut a long murder story short, the only things Virgo willingly spends his and/or your money on are personal grooming kits for him, household cleaning products for you and, yes, those infernal icepicks.

HOW TO SPOT ONE
If he looks vaguely familiar, that's because he is. You probably saw an artist's sketchy impression on *Crime Spotters* the night before and faintly remember words like 'bludgeoned', 'manhunt' and 'Virgo'. However, he's much more attractive in the flesh. He's well groomed and often fair of hair – like most serial killers in most killer serials. Just look for the cool, calm, collected one doing nothing but staring disconcertingly at you from across the room.

How to Spot a B*st*rd by his Star Sign

Holding up bank queues querying bank charges. Loitering outside self-motivation seminars. Loitering inside the Army Reserves. In a public lavatory wiping the evidence off his hands. In a maximum security psychiatric ward complaining the wardens put his jacket on back to front and, furthermore, it doesn't go with his trousers.

HOW TO INTRIGUE ONE

Mention your inheritance in casual conversation. At the same time run your finger seductively up and down the bar counter and comment upon the disgraceful amount of dust there.

THE FIRST DATE

When he eventually gets around to asking you out, he'll take you to one of those Hare Krishna centres where for less than 50 pence you can have all the lentils you do not wish to eat. (*Handy hint: don't insincerely offer to split the bill unless you genuinely want to get rid of all the small change in the bottom of your handbag.*) Be on your guard if, towards the end of the evening, he says he knows this great little spot for an after-dinner drink and it happens to be down a cellar, atop a cliff or up a dark alley.

WHEN TO DO THE DEED

Don't. The Virgo bastard does for sex what Hannibal Lector did for the Beef and Livestock Corporation.

WHEN TO POP THE QUESTION

What question are we talking about here? 'When you polish

your faucet in future can you also remember to clean the bathtub?', 'How come I'm paying for dinner again?' or 'Why do you wax the hair on your chest when you've got so little on your head?'.

IF HE DROPS YOU

Like most things in Virgo's life, he'll probably never get around to it. If he does, it's obviously because you didn't keep his shower recess clean enough or file his grocery receipts properly. Either that or you flicked through the mug-shots at the local police station, pointed to his face and said: 'That's him. That's the low-life who *loaned* me 40 pence to make an emergency phone call after he attempted to hack me to death.'

IF YOU DROP HIM

He'll be ominously, quietly hurt. And just when you think you're rid of him, he'll appear from behind, accompanied by dodgy camera angles and predictable cello solo. Don't think he's hiding a bunch of flowers behind his back – flowers cost money. No, the thing in his hand behind his back is that goddamned icepick again.

The Capricorn Bastard

22 DECEMBER–20 JANUARY

Finally, a man who takes relationships seriously. Blessed with the sensitivity of a security analyst, the humour of an IBM clone and the heart of a merchant banker, a Capricorn takes *everything* seriously.

His intentions towards you are entirely honourable. He is hard-working and ambitious. He wants to get married and raise a family. He has no problem with the concept and implementation of commitment. He'll even be faithful to you – although this can't be guaranteed as he *is* a man.

And upon getting to know him better you'll find he also possesses all the charm and conversation of a cash register. (Well, you can't expect him to have all those virtues *and* a personality.) But before you jump up and down in orgiastic delight at the thought of spending time with him, there is a catch. There's something he has to do prior to whisking you off into the sunset to issue joint financial statements together: he has to check your credit rating. And no, he's not joking. He never jokes about money. Or anything else come to think of it.

If you happened to be born with silver cutlery anywhere near your mouth and you have a large inheritance threatening to fall in your lap, you're laughing (and he may even smile) all the way to the bank and the joint savings account. However, don't assume he's only interested in you for your inheritance. Such an assumption would be a gross misjudgment of character. The truth is, if you'd won the money in a lottery or made it yourself through hard work or shrewd investments, he'd still be interested in you.

It would be unfair to say money is the only thing that matters to Capricorn. He is mostly human and understands your money alone will not ensure his happiness. That's why your social status is just as important to him. He'll not only be interested in you for what you have but for who you are, who you know, who your parents are, what they have and who they know. (And you thought men were only interested in *one* thing.) Anyway, he's not searching for the love of his life. He first found that as a small child, beneath the cushions of his parents' couch. And he will always be true to it. Besides, marriage isn't about love. It's about making money.

Capricorn is the reason finishing schools still exist. You know, those wonderfully traditional educational institutions that concern themselves with taking affluent, intelligent young women and making them completely useless for anything other than marriage. As well as offering the only recognised diploma course in *Understanding Cutlery 101*, these outrageously expensive and usually Swiss schools take all the hard work out of finding a partner for Capricorn.

The cost involved ensures only the very wealthy and socially well placed can afford to send their daughters there. This eliminates all unsuitable candidates. Then the suitable are vigorously trained to eliminate any beliefs they may have in gender equality or themselves.

First you learn to cook the kind of meals which take days or sometimes weeks of preparation – the results of which can be ruined in a few seconds by an aeroplane passing overhead. This is to keep you occupied after you are married and is also impressive when you have to throw dinner parties for your Capricorn-bastard-husband's business contacts.

Then you'll learn to cultivate/fake an appreciation of the arts and an understanding of politics and world affairs so you can make seemingly intelligent conversation whilst you are cooking for and serving the guests. At these dinner parties you could translate a business deal for your husband with one of the five major European languages you picked up between classes at finishing school. And as for the etiquette required to know exactly where at the table to seat an earl or a prime minister if a member of the royal family is also coming – well, that was covered in your first year when you studied *Introduction to Seating Royalty, Nobility and Important Public Officials*.

Along with *How to Lose a Tennis Match to a Man Without Him Suspecting You are Throwing the Game to Save his Ego, The Art of Table Setting II (Advanced Course), How to Be Patronised Gracefully* and countless other vital business courses, you will be taught to walk, to speak and to dress yourself properly. Sure, you may have learnt to do these things when you were 18 months old but these schools don't take any chances. You will also be taught needlework – majoring in embroidery. We have no idea why.

But the most important thing you can do at these schools is to mix and become lifelong friends with all those other obscenely rich, pedigreed girls. You don't actually have to like them, you just have to kiss the air around their cheeks for the rest of your life. They, like you, will go on to marry Capricorn bastards to whom you can introduce your Capricorn bastard. These bastards will then form a boys' club where they can compare penis sizes (though they'll call it networking) to their hearts' content. Naturally, you won't be allowed to join as you don't have a penis and, as you're married to a Capricorn bastard, you'll only ever get one at the end of each financial year – if it was a successful one.

You are now a graduate of the you-can-never-be-too-thin-too-rich-too-blonde-or-too-tanned school of thought and you are accomplished enough to take up that all-important position of catering to Capricorn's whims. You're a perfect wife: you have absolutely no marketable skills so you'll have nothing better to do than to further your husband's career. In other words, you will be *bored*. In your perfect house with your perfect husband and your perfect children. Bored with your air-and-arse-kissing friends who are all as boring as you. Bored with all the affairs you've had with the hired help because your husband only has sex if the Windsor-Kennedy-Smythe-Joneses are doing it too (and they never get around to it either). Bored, blonde, rich and eminently socially acceptable. May we suggest slipping into a coma to get through it all. No one will ever notice the difference.

NB: In more astrologically qualified circles there are a couple of widely repeated rumours about Capricorn. Firstly, deep down, he is reported to have the romantic soul of a poet – though we find this hard to believe. And secondly, once he achieves his financial and social ambitions and retires, he becomes a lot of fun to have around. We can neither deny nor confirm this as we think life is too short to spend it with a Capricorn bastard.

HOW TO SPOT ONE
Sneak a look under his bed to find his favourite well-thumbed and stained copies of the *Harvard Business Review*.

WHERE TO FIND ONE
At graduation ceremonies at finishing schools. In buildings where large sums of money are stored. Scanning the social pages for recently separated women with impressive names and even more impressive divorce settlements.

How to Spot a B*st*rd by his Star Sign

HOW TO INTRIGUE ONE

Accidentally drop your investment portfolio (the one embossed with your heavily hyphenated name) and make sure it is substantial enough to register on the Richter scale when it hits the ground. As he is helping you retrieve it, spill some large denomination notes into his lap whilst also dropping the names of all the big important people that Daddy-the-media-magnate-or-hotel-tycoon-or-reigning-monarch-of-a-small-but-wealthy-and-tax-free-nation wants to introduce your future husband to.

THE FIRST DATE

He will use this first meeting to assess your suitability; to figure out whether or not you are worth the investment; to see if you know the difference between a fish fork and a dessert fork. In fact it'll be a lot like a job interview. (*Tip: Make sure you look like a million dollars. At least.*)

WHEN TO DO THE DEED

Go snooping in his Filofax. He'll have it scheduled in. Or better yet, ask his secretary when he plans to seal the deal – she'll have a clearer idea of when he can fit himself in. (Important note: The Capricorn bastard is quite good at sex. He passed *Sleeping Your Way to the Top I & II & III* with flying colours. It's amazing what they teach you at business schools these days.)

WHEN TO POP THE QUESTION

When you own at least 51 per cent of his corporation. He's not going to refuse his major shareholder. And, even if he does, you have the deciding vote – so you can overrule him.

IF HE DROPS YOU
This is a very good sign. It means he's getting serious about you. He's starting to negotiate. Have Daddy up the dowry and go back with a counter offer.

IF YOU DROP HIM
He's financially secure enough to handle it. It's all there in the pre-nuptial agreement; the dowry was non-refundable in the event of disagreement. As for the rest of your inheritance – well, he'll just have to marry another retirement plan.

We-Love-You-We-Love-You-Not

AIR SIGNS

Gemini, Libra, Aquarius

Possessing a remarkable inability to stick to anything for long,
Air Sign Bastards make incredibly poor long-term partners and
even poorer wall-hangings. They have little or no idea how to
conduct themselves in a relationship and only have a vague
inkling of what a relationship actually is. Yet this doesn't prevent
them from trying to pass themselves off on the unsuspecting,
astrologically unaware as suitable lovers and partners.

Air Sign Bastards are game to try anything once. For a short
time. But ask them to commit to anything longer than a lunch
and they'll literally disappear into thin air. They were born with

55

an innate fear of commitment and, more importantly, an ability to sense its looming presence far enough away to always stay one step ahead of its clutches.

So, it stands to reason: if you require attentiveness, sympathy or even just the physical presence of partners, don't go running to Air Sign Bastards. Firstly, you won't be able to catch them. Secondly, they're not really interested in getting to know you any better. Though it's not that they don't care enough. It's just that they don't care at all.

The bummer is, Air Sign Bastards lack the vital organ – a heart – necessary for you to inflict emotional trauma upon them and they are never around long enough for you to attempt lasting physical harm.

The Gemini Bastard

22 May–21 June

Relationships just don't hold much appeal for a Gemini bastard. The hours are terribly inconvenient. Intimacy is stifling. Monogamy sucks. Rules are stupid. And as for the thought of spending time alone with you – that's absolutely terrifying. See, you could get too close. Then you'd want to know what's deep down inside of him. And he's afraid to show you because he's not quite sure what's down there himself. (Our bets are on a primordial black hole.) This is why he'll prefer to keep you as just an acquaintance. Even after you're married to him.

But there's good reason for his behaviour: *he's possessed*. No, don't call the exorcist. This isn't a medieval chant, holy water and crucifix thing. It's worse. A Gemini bastard has many demons – a multitude of personalities living inside him, each of whom qualifies as a bastard in his own right.

Firstly, there's Mikey. He gets to go first because he has the earliest bedtime. He's eternally four years old and alternates between a total cherub and the brat from hell – the former when he's asleep and the latter when he's awake. He makes all the major financial, family and relationship decisions. In fact he handles everything of importance. When the rare occasion arises on which he needs advice he turns to Zoltan (see next page). Otherwise he is a normal four-year-old – incapable of taking care of himself. Spending time with him is like any normal four-year-old play session: it usually ends in tears. Your tears. Of sheer frustration.

A psychiatrist would probably diagnose Mikey as a symptom of the fact Gemini doesn't want to grow up and take responsibility for his life. Whether or not this is true, Mikey is a minor and as such cannot be held responsible for his actions either by you or the law.

Next up is Tony, a real piece of work. He's a used car salesman. A very, very good one. He's the reason you're in a relationship with a Gemini bastard in the first place. He's very good at selling things nobody wants. When you confront Gemini and tell him you don't believe he (sob) truly cares about you, Tony jumps in with something along the lines of: 'But Sarah, the idea of life without you is inconceivable to me. You are my reason for living, the most important person in my world,' etc. He'll seem so sincere and convincing you'll believe him, even though your name is Rachel.

How to Spot a B*st*rd by his Star Sign

Oh, and have you met Frank? You'll just *love* Frank. He works the room for a living. He's the life and soul of a double-vodka-martini cocktail party. He's intensely interested in people other than you. For up to five minutes at a time. If he seems superficial, that's only because he is. The 'other people' adore Frank and invite him everywhere, encouraging him to be even more annoying.

Walter, on the other hand, is dreadfully unpopular. He's nervous, jumpy and always in need of a good stiff drink. He appears whenever there's a tense or stressful situation and runs around making an awful commotion without actually being of any use.

Charles is infinitely more useful. A brilliant prosecuting attorney always is. Whenever Gemini finds he has painted himself into a corner (and you think you've finally pinned him down) Charles comes to the rescue. He is logical, cynical and heartless. He can make you admit to committing crimes you've never even heard of. Unfortunately for justice, he uses his formidable talent to prosecute the victim. And in the case of dating Gemini, you are *always* the victim.

Last and least is Zoltan. Master Sorcerer, Dragon Slayer, Defender of the Universe and Keeper of the Legendary Golden Orb (the one with the sticker that says, 'For use in the event of the complete destruction of mankind. Press blue button to save world. If you feel like it.'). We aren't really sure where Zoltan fits in. He is officially in charge of changing light bulbs, refilling ice-cube trays and other light domestic chores (but, naturally, a man on whom the fate of the entire universe depends can't be expected to be good at mundane details). We also suspect he's the one responsible for listening when wives and girlfriends want to 'talk'.

So now you know it's not that your Gemini bastard doesn't care about you, it's just that Zoltan is limited in what he can do to resolve your problems when he exists in another reality. Once you get those earthly problems out into deep space, they look kind of small and insignificant. And just how practical can you expect someone named Zoltan to be? (*Warning: Zoltan has been known to make the leap across the space-time continuum to go out on dates.*)

Mikey, Tony, Frank, Walter, Charles and Zoltan all interact with one another. They egg each other on, whip each other into mad frenzies and appear in random order to torment you. The medical term for this is Multiple Personality Disorder.

Because Gemini lives amid this turmoil he will continually change his ideas and opinions. What he says today won't mean anything tomorrow and it probably didn't mean much today either. You could see this as a natural result of him having to deal with his conflicting personalities. Or you could see it as a result of him being a two-faced, two-timing, lying bastard. But, thankfully, there are a few things guaranteed to remain constant in your Gemini bastard. These things are the traits all his personalities have in common. They are never ever wrong. They are never ever at fault. and they will never ever have an attention span of longer than 15 seconds.

So if Gemini plans to go to the movies with you a week ahead of time and actually follows through, see it as long-term commitment (sorry, this is as good as it gets) and send out the wedding invitations.

Once you are married and you decide you and the kids would really like to see your Gemini bastard more than once a week – though most likely this will be enough – all is not lost. Just get work experience as a warden in a maximum security facility where the inmates are constantly trying to escape. Then you'll know how to deal with him. Or pack up the family and move to Alcatraz. They'll put you in separate cells but at least you'll know where your Gemini bastard is at all times.

How to spot one
Gemini is particularly hard to spot. He'll be standing in front of you, talking at you in one instant and he'll be a blur in the distance the next. This is a real problem if you want to shoot him.

Where to find one
On television chat shows, on psychiatrists' couches, on the phone to recorded-message services or at a McDonald's drive-through having an interesting discussion with the intercom. Basically, anywhere he can have a conversation without making an emotional commitment.

How to intrigue one
Don't require sympathy. Or consistency. Or fidelity. Or company. Don't ask where he is going. Or when he might be coming back. Or if he is coming back. And don't ever ask anything more emotionally demanding than 'How are you?' or 'Where did you get your shoes?'

The first date
Enjoy it. He will actually pay attention to you as he isn't bored with you yet. (*Tip: To prolong his interest, try not to wear clothing more interesting than you are.*)

WHEN TO DO THE DEED

As soon as possible. How often do you get the chance to indulge in group sex? (All Gemini's personalities take part in sex. This means he doesn't have to have an emotional obligation to you as you're technically sleeping with other people.)

WHEN TO POP THE QUESTION

At times you'll see that, not-so-deep-down, Gemini is truly committed to you. Like when he manages – without the help of cue cards – to remember the names of your three children. This is as good a time as any to bring up marriage. And unless you want your kids to resent you for not managing to marry their father within their lifetime, don't be too demanding. Holding out until he manages to put the right name to the right child is asking far too much.

IF HE DROPS YOU

It doesn't mean he doesn't like you any more. He's just forgotten you, that's all. If you really miss him, engineer a chance meeting. You'll pique his interest as he'll find you vaguely familiar, reminding him of someone . . . hmmm . . . whom he can't quite place. Then you can start dating him all over again.

IF YOU DROP HIM

Gemini will suddenly discover he definitely does have deep feelings for you. Feelings you have hurt. Terribly. Irrevocably. His heart is shattered. His soul destroyed. His life meaningless. How could you do this to him, you . . . you . . . *what was your name again?*

The Libra Bastard

The poor, confused bastard. It's not *his* fault. Life in the modern world is getting more and more complex and there are so many *decisions* to make. He now has to decide between a half-flush and a full-flush every time he goes to the toilet. The stress is *unbelievable*.

So you can just imagine the pressure he's under when he has to decide whether or not to ask you out. What if he does discover he really likes you and wants to see you again? What if he sees you again and likes you even more? Then he'd have to keep on seeing you. Which would probably lead to a major commitment like marriage and kids. And he's not quite sure where to take the family on their annual holiday or where the boys should go to school.

What if you aren't the love of his life, but he marries you anyway? Then what would he do when the real love of his life comes along? What if he doesn't ask you out, and you turn out to be the woman of his dreams? Then he would spend his whole life knowing he let you go. So maybe he should ask you out just in case. But, then again, maybe it's better not to see the woman of his dreams on a daily basis because that would make it all so mundane and not a bit romantic.

And there's another thing to consider: *what if he asks you out and you say 'no'?*

It's a wonder Libra ever ends up in a relationship at all. But the truth is, he's always sort-of-involved or looking to be sort-of-involved. He wanders aimlessly from relationship to relationship, getting himself into situations which don't stand a chance; trying to find understanding with a 16-year-old schoolgirl; having a baby with someone he only sees once every six months; living with someone who lives in another county; and so on. (Seven out of ten dead-end relationships involve a Libra bastard. The other three mainly concern Pisces bastards.)

All the while, Libra is hoping the right girl will come along and make a decision for him. And even if *she* never comes along, he's sort-of-sure there's someone better than you just around the corner. It's a real pity he doesn't just go and look around the corner. Because in the relationship (which you've semi-convinced him he'd like to keep) there are other things to occupy his overworked little mind. Things that have to do with you; like whether or not you're keeping yourself attractive enough for him; whether or not you've put on weight; whether or not he finds your voice grating.

Of course, at the start of a relationship he'll never voice any of these worries. Somehow you'll just *know* you're doing something wrong. It does help to have heightened perception, though. Or just the ability to apologise profusely for anything you ever say or do.

On a lighter note, at least you'll never have to worry about him questioning your integrity or the beliefs you hold dear. Let's just say that if Libra was a swimming-pool there wouldn't be a deep end. His concerns about you only ever have to do with the way you look, sound, dress or act.

But whilst your innermost feelings are safely beyond Libra's comprehension, your numerous surface flaws will receive more and more of his attention. And when he thinks he's put up with the latter for long enough, he'll change them by hinting and harping and whining until you're forced to give in without even the satisfaction of a good old-fashioned fist-fight.

If you do put on what he considers to be an excessive display of emotion, he'll just strategically withdraw, making you look like a screaming shrew whilst he looks oh-so-bloody-reasonable. Then, when you've stopped screaming and sobbing and smashing crockery, he'll be back once more to hint and harp and whine again. And again. And again. You'll soon learn to give in at the start because it saves so much time. Face facts here: the Libra bastard always gets his own way.

Before you know it, the two of you will be doing things only he wants to do, seeing people only he wants to see, and going to places only he wants to go. So if there is anything in your life that's actually important to you – like your career, for instance – try and get less attached to it. In no time, you'll be wondering where the smooth Libran charmer you started dating went.

In fact, he didn't go anywhere – that would require making a decision. He was just an optical illusion. The intolerant, exacting creep you now know and love is frighteningly real. He will judge your behaviour against outrageous standards that he wouldn't dream of using on himself. You'll be expected to take out the swimsuit and evening gown sections of the Miss World pageant as well as walking away with the Ms Congeniality title. And you'll also be required to combine these skills with those of a gourmet chef and interior designer. Once you've achieved all of this he will happily take you for granted. Well, for a while, at least. Until he notices all the new flaws you've developed as a result of your new skills.

On the up-side you'll find that the two of you will spend a lot of time in the bathroom together – though you'll have to stand in line for the hairdrier and mirror. And in the bedroom his clothes will probably take up most of the closet space (but this is a good thing as it won't leave room for the skeletons of old girlfriends he's not sure he's finished with yet he'll want to hide there).

Just make sure you compliment him regularly on his youthful good looks, cater to his every whim, keep yourself nice and don't ask questions that require an answer. Keep these simple things in mind and you can't go wrong. Whilst you're at it, try not to act coarse or say anything in bad taste. It'll only set him wondering again whether or not he made the right decision to ask you out in the first place.

HOW TO SPOT ONE
He's the charmingly boyish, well-dressed one standing in the corner – near the mirror, trying to make up his mind as to whether he should approach you. You can be absolutely sure he is a Libra bastard if his decision takes more than a day.

WHERE TO FIND ONE
At forks in the road, in modern, dual-flushing toilets or on the judging panel of a Ms Universe contest. In fact, anywhere there are trivial decisions to be made.

HOW TO INGRIGUE ONE
Appear to know who you are and where you are going. Appear to be Cindy Crawford fresh from a Revlon shoot. Appear to be carefree and unused to heavy thoughts. Appear to be his mother. Then wait with the patience of an angel for him to make a move.

How to Spot a B*st*rd by his Star Sign

THE FIRST DATE

The first date with Libra is usually quite wonderful. He'll take you to a popular place where the wine (you chose it), wit (yours, that is) and conversation (yours again) will flow. He'll even pick up the bill with a generous flourish (he's seen other men do it). So why *did* you have to go and spoil it all by asking if he's going to call you again?

WHEN TO DO THE DEED

Hold out as long as possible – it's not like you'll be missing anything. Stretch it out for a year or two whilst he's busy deciding whether or not to date you. In any case, it'll end up being your decision and therefore your fault.

WHEN TO POP THE QUESTION

When you want the relationship to end.

IF HE DROPS YOU

This means he has met somebody else as he's incapable of ending a relationship without help from a grown-up. If you try and get him back, it'll just confuse him. Whether or not he goes or stays, he'll claim you forced him into the decision. Best to leave well enough alone.

IF YOU DROP HIM

Libra will be settled, happily or not, with a new partner before the ink is dry on the Dear (insert-appropriate-Standard-Boy's-Name-here) letter you send him. You could feel outraged at the speed in which he forgets you. Then again you'll find it impossible to continue to take him that seriously.

The Aquarius Bastard

21 JANUARY–19 FEBRUARY

Aquarius is the most reasonable bastard you'll ever encounter. He'll even agree he is a bastard. If he was born out of wedlock then he is one by definition and if you want to call him a bastard for other, more personal, reasons he'll certainly allow you your opinion.

And he won't, like other bastards and real astrologers, dismiss this book as amateur astrological crap. In his mind every viewpoint gets a hearing, every belief system has some legitimacy. To top things off, he's likely to be annoyingly good-looking (well there goes your ability to remain objective). Cuteness aside, open-mindedness and tolerance in a bastard has its own set of problems. A very different set of problems than you're used to. In fact, after years of dealing with men who don't listen to you when the football, the television or the fridge is on, you'll be totally unequipped to deal with Aquarius.

Standard forms of male manipulation (e.g. screaming like a banshee or carefully planned sex deprivation) don't work on Aquarius. He is more profound and more complex than the average bastard. Whilst normal little boys were constructing little Lego spacecraft piloted by little Lego spacemen from the planet Biffo, Aquarius junior was delving into the mysteries of existence. True, he did it via television and comic books, but his sincere intention to discover the deeper meaning of life was there. The distressing thing is he managed to find depth and reality in *The Brady Bunch* and in the Bat Cave and will regale you with their profundity.

Spending his formative years as a weirdo has resulted in the adult Aquarius male holding radical beliefs. Being a radical is quite easy. He doesn't have to stick to one system of thought as, say, the poor communists do. He can adopt an ideology to fit his mood and situation. And he'll be happy as long as it allows him to oppose some commonly held belief – your belief in marriage, for instance.

Taking the opposing stance is the foundation of all his beliefs. And once everybody else is a radical, left-wing, feminist-separatist-greenie-with-a-nose-ring, he'll became a radical conservative. The only thing he hates more than conservatism is to do what everybody else is doing. He prides himself on his otherness.

It follows, then, that his views on romantic relationships defy conventions and escape comprehension. See, commitment limits personal growth for both partners. Marriage is an outmoded aspect of organised religion and is no more than a pricey piece of paper in today's world, and love (like currency) should be circulated for the benefit of everybody – not hoarded in a miserly way to be doled out regularly to one individual.

Of course, that one individual – you, in this case – may have different thoughts on the matter. In theory, his beliefs are fine. There is nothing wrong with seeing each human being as a free and responsible agent determining their own path through life. It's just not terribly warm and fuzzy. And it presents some practical difficulties. Like, where do you, the station wagon and the two-point-three children fit in?

That's a huge problem with most philosophers – they don't include a section entitled 'How to Nab a Man and Keep Him' in their manifestos. (They haven't included other basic human needs either – like clothes, shopping and trashy television shows.)

Understandably, you'll come to the conclusion Aquarius is operating on a completely different, totally baffling level. But the thing is, he does believe in love. The all-encompassing kind. The noble feeling of compassion for one's fellow men – which unites people for the greater good of humanity. The selfless, undemanding emotion . . . (sorry, we have to stop here – we're feeling slightly nauseous). And of course he loves you. Aren't you a fellow inhabitant of earth? How could he *not* love you?

What Aquarius fails to understand is that loving all human beings equally only ever worked for Jesus Christ, and Jesus Christ was quite an extraordinary person. How secure are you going to feel dating a mere mortal who practises this? And as Aquarius is busy spreading his love among humanity, you can't even cause a scene about it. Making a fuss would mean you were jealous. And jealousy is a primitive, self-destructive emotion. You must have an incredibly low opinion of yourself to even entertain such a feeling – you really do have some major self-doubts, don't you? Perhaps you should discuss this problem of yours with Aquarius because he really does want to help.

That's the problem, Aquarius has noble, humane reasons for everything he does. Reasons which make you look selfish and uncaring for putting your needs before those whose needs are greater than your own. Shame on you. When was the last time *you* built a well for a Third World village? (Although now and then, amongst his great rhetoric, you'll get a sneaking feeling all of this is just an elaborate hoax designed to cover up his fear of commitment.)

You can't even nail your Aquarius bastard for sexism – he'll show you up. He's read all those books you bought to place on your shelf for decorative purposes. He'll dismiss your rantings as a product of the victim feminism so prevalent these days and so damaging to the real feminist cause.

Face it, he's a better feminist than you are. He's spent years pondering the male paradox (i.e. how can one be male, loaded up with testosterone and still be a decent human being?). Hence his evasive, noncommital behaviour towards you. He's actually trying to make up for all that his gender has done. The less time he spends with you the less chance he has to undermine your gender by treating you like an unpaid domestic servant – as men are biologically inclined to do. And he won't be guilty of treating you as a sex object if he doesn't have sex with you regularly. Instead, he can spread his natural male instinct to objectify women over a number of them thus diluting its damaging effect. See how concerned he is about you? Are you feeling grateful yet?

Well, if you aren't, don't get any bright ideas about trying to talk your Aquarius bastard around to your point of view. You'll be up against the arguments of Plato, Kant, Jung, Gandhi, Dr Seuss and every other great-though-male mind of human civilisation. And, frankly, you and your PhD in Nagging from the College of Applied Domestic Arts and Sciences can't quite cut it in this league.

HOW TO SPOT ONE
Find him attractive and he'll be completely oblivious to your

existence. Ignore him and he'll be all over you. Yes, we know, we've just described the behaviour of almost any man – so also look for an unhealthy gleam in his eye (as seen in the eyes of Born-Again Christians or people who live in small, padded rooms with locks on the outside).

WHERE TO FIND ONE
Look in the exalted circles of Nobel laureates, inventors-of-things-that-help-mankind and great humanitarians to find your very own Aquarius bastard. If this fails, look in the nearest looney bin. There are even more of them to choose from here.

HOW TO INTRIGUE ONE
Talk about some really interesting things you've done; like the time you restored peace in the Middle East; how you invented a cure for cancer; or when you discovered and communicated with a new form of life in the next galaxy – stuff like that. (*Tip: In general conversation, try not to come across as too ideologically unsound.*)

THE FIRST DATE
It probably won't be a 'date' as such. He's much more interested in you as a person and will ask you out on that pretext. After a few friendly encounters he'll notice you are a girl – you can then move things along from there.

WHEN TO DO THE DEED
There is no need to abide by convention for this or any other aspect of your dealings with Aquarius. But do it discreetly so he

doesn't notice. He'd hate to think he was taking advantage of you. (*NB: To save you from disappointment, be aware that when Aquarius mentioned The Big Bang Theory he wasn't referring to his sexual performance.*)

WHEN TO POP THE QUESTION

Never, under any circumstances, do this. It will alert him to the fact you think of the relationship as more than just friendship. However, if you happen to be a member of an oppressed minority group, you stand a good chance of getting an Aquarian bastard to the altar – he won't want to be guilty of discrimination.

IF HE DROPS YOU

He'll never really drop you. He'll always value you as a person. He'll just stop having sex with you – so the relationship won't change really.

IF YOU DROP HIM

He'll take it philosophically and figure it was for the best anyway. But he'll ask if you can still be friends and won't be able to understand why you slam the door/hang up the phone/shoot him in the kneecap.

Don't-Hate-Us-'Cos-We're-Wishy-Washy

WATER SIGNS

Cancer, Scorpio, Pisces

For 'deep, sensitive and sensual' read 'secretive, paranoid and seriously perverted'. Water Sign Bastards are to be avoided at all costs. They're deceitful, highly strung deviants who are hard to pin down except to a mattress.

Yes, Water Sign Bastards *can* be very deep, sensitive and sensual. Because they're so *deep* they can look within themselves and see what wretched failures they truly are. Because they're so *sensitive* they're acutely aware women neither like nor respect them. And because they're so *sensual*, they'll make sure you feel their torment too. This is fine if you're a seriously co-dependent type who likes feeling maladjusted all the time. Because, in a pathetic attempt to bolster their own self-esteem, Water Sign Bastards end up sucking every last drop of self-respect out of you. Without you, they're nothing. Of course, with you they're nothing either. But that's beside the point.

Fortunately for you, Water Sign Bastards have very strong suicidal tendencies. Equally as unfortunately for you is that whilst they are wont to sit on top of very high kerbs and threaten to jump off, they never have the guts or good manners to follow through.

The Cancer Bastard

22 June–23 July

Dear Mother,

I hope you are well. I am doing fine but wish you were here. A weekend away seems such a long time. Have just met a girl who I think could be the one. Like you, she is really pretty and really nice. I am sure the two of you will get on like a house on fire.

Your ever-devoted son,
Cancer.

Well, we couldn't have put it better ourselves. You're the house, she's the fire. And guess which one of you ends up the worst for wear?

To be fair, though, every mother openly loves her son and therefore secretly resents his girlfriend. In return, every son secretly loves his mother and openly resents his girlfriend. But any boy should have the decency to look visibly embarrassed when mummy combs his hair and wipes his face with a hanky laced with her own spit. When he's *thirty-eight*.

However, we're not talking about a grown man here, are we? Were talking about Cancer. So, if you've just fallen in love with one, best of luck. Hopefully the old bag is dead. Because if she is still rattling around, you don't stand a bloody chance. The Cancer bastard's relationship with mother is the keystone to his existence. His ties to the apron strings make Oedipus look like a well-balanced, independent type who left home at an early age and only occasionally remembered to send his mother a birthday card.

Either Cancer dotes on mother to death and no other women can come betwixt, or else he hates her guts and therefore detests that 51 per cent of the population capable of bearing children.

It's probably better he leans towards the latter because that way he'll be so repellent you won't want to go anywhere near him. Unfortunately, he's more likely to be trotting over to her coven on a regular basis, affording her the opportunity to watch every wrong move you make. And let us tell you now: *you won't be good enough for her son*. Which she will tell him. And then tell him to tell you. This is often why Cancer will put off introductions between the two of you for as long as possible, and it is the only aspect of his widespread gutlessness to be applauded and, indeed, encouraged.

To your face, Cancer's mother will be as sweet as pie. But when you've looked beyond the wart on the end of her nose and begun to watch very, very closely, you'll soon realise where the term son-of-a-bitch comes from.

She'll generously load your plate with kilos of kilojoules in the hope you'll end up as fat as her. Then, after you politely refuse a second helping, she'll kindly inquire after your eating disorder.

When Cancer – who is in his high-chair at the kitchen bench toying with his mashed steak away from the adults – looks certain to leap to your defence, she'll fix him with the kind of glare that makes you all of a sudden want to reach for the dictionary and find out what a 'gimlet' actually is.

She'll subliminally click her tongue when you let him get up to wash his own bowl and spoon. It goes without saying she'll be silently apoplectic when you pass him your plate to wash also. When she can bring herself to speak again, she will innocently ask you why women of today can never seem to hold on to their men. This will prompt you to wonder why you haven't yet seen hide or hair of Cancer's father. (Popular myth says the Cancer bastard didn't have a father. Common legend has it he was spawned. Stark reality deems dad died years ago of filial disappointment.)

As things are now beginning to get a bit strained between you and her, Cancer will pull one of his infamous panic attacks. This translates into a very mild fever, the faintest hint of the tremors, a few tears for dramatic effect and an inability to finish whatever he's doing at the time.

You won't help matters much by callously standing by whilst mother rushes to his side, clears his air passage of any obstructions, does a quick Heimlich Manoeuvre and whips the sponge out of his shaking hands to do the dishes for him.

How were you to know about the dark family secret? No one told you Cancer was struck down at a tragically young age with mad cow's disease, now more popularly known as mother-who-molly-coddles. To date, your idea of babying an adult male has been to chuck him a codeine capsule as you waltz out the door to that all-important meeting or party.

So aggrieved you haven't given him the milk of human kindness he so richly deserves and mother still provides by way of bottled formula, Cancer will proceed to do what he does best and have a 'mood'. The huffs, puffs and sulks of Cancer make his namesake seem like a really fun thing to have around. And just when you think the thing's in remission, he'll scowl for a change of scenery. Don't be tempted to ask what's wrong because he'll just say 'nothing'. Mother specifically told him not to talk to strangers. And, be reasonable, he's hardly had time to get to know you over the last three years, what with all that self-introspection he's had to do.

The only way to make amends is to buy him a really fabulous present on the way home – preferably something old and precious so he can be reminded of you-know-who. Naturally if this can't be arranged, just slip him a cheque.

In order to keep him in the sheltered lifestyle she believes to be his birthright, Cancer's mother never charged him board. Therefore Cancer has learnt over the years to enjoy hoarding money. And, since the brain-addled bat also discouraged him from being ambitious enough to get a well-paid career when he grew up (because then he might flee the nest), he's had to be extraordinarily mean in order to accumulate a lot of it.

On the off-chance he does lash out on you (a box of home brand chocolates is always an encouraging sign), he'll be so racked with worry about his profligate spending he'll secretly hold it against you for months. So if he does grudgingly proffer an extravagant gift, express your eternal gratitude, discreetly return it to the discount store from whence it came and surreptitiously deposit the money back into his bank account.

Of course, this is precisely what he wanted you to do but was too afraid to ask because then you might scold him for being a sneaky, selfish little brat and just wait till you tell his mother. If there's one thing he's more terrified of than being upfront, it's the thought of *her* walking steadily towards him with grim expression and heavy wooden coathanger.

HOW TO SPOT ONE
The grown man with the attributes of a vile child is invariably Cancer. If he's also wearing a nappy, back off. He's either too young for you – or too old.

WHERE TO FIND ONE
In a bookstore asking for directions to the self-help section; in a Good Samaritan bin shopping for your birthday present; out drinking with the lads just to prove he's one of them (however, one alcoholic beverage too many [one] and he'll be whingeing about how hard it ish to find a woman who can live up to hish mothersh expectashuns).

HOW TO INTRIGUE ONE
Tell him you like his mother. Tell him you like him. Or be honest, straightforward and positive and tell both of them to drop dead.

THE FIRST DATE
He'll invite you over to dinner and cook for you because it's

cheaper than going out. On the rare occasion he invites you to his mother's place, it'll only be because he still lives there.

WHEN TO DO THE DEED
When he's declared his undying love. Which he will. Very quickly. He's a two-fingers-down-the-throat romantic who used to steal glances at his mother's Barbara Cartland novels when normal boys were shoplifting *Hustler.* Just don't be surprised when he takes it back again the next morning – particularly after mother bangs on the bedroom door and asks if he's all right because she heard him moaning and groaning through the night and thought he might have an upset tummy.

WHEN TO POP THE QUESTION
Never, ever, *ever* marry a Cancer bastard. Or else you'll be forced to become his surrogate mother because that's the only way you'll get his attention and her goat.

IF HE DROPS YOU
He's doing you a big favour and since favours aren't his forte, you should be grateful. Of course, because the Cancer bastard doesn't like being alone with himself for too long (and who can blame him) he's bound to come crawling back.

IF YOU DROP HIM
He'll run bawling to mummy and she'll make him demand back the presents he bought you with her pension – but you didn't want that *Cookery in 1,000 Easy Lessons* book anyway, did you?

The Scorpio Bastard

24 OCTOBER–22 NOVEMBER

All those dark, brooding, monosyllabic types who fill the pages of cheap romance novels with their strong jaws and piercing eyes are Scorpios. You know the story: boy meets girl. Boy tortures girl because of a series of very silly misunderstandings and because he enjoys it. Girl becomes a psychological wreck. Boy sweeps girl into his arms and mumbles something about undying love. (He has to sweep her into his arms because by this stage the poor woman has completely fallen apart.)

This is where the book ends. There is a very good reason for this. Mills & Boon know what is to come is far too awful to be published.

Yet this paperback ideal of love still manages to override the common sense of most women. We find the strong, silent, manipulative type irresistible. And we sit prettily on our hope chests with our long auburn curls in charming disarray, waiting breathlessly with much fluttering of eyelashes for Scorpio to *stride* into our lives. (*NB: Romantic heroes never walk, they always stride – manfully and purposefully. It's dreadfully tiring for them and it is one of the reasons why they are so moody and irritable.*)

And once a Scorpio bastard arrives? Well, there's nothing like a spot of good-old-fashioned-bodice-ripping to get things started. Just swoon gracefully into his arms and let him have his wicked way with you. Then have your head examined. The strong, silent type is what you should look for when purchasing white goods. Whilst these are desirable attributes in a washing machine, you won't enjoy them in Scorpio.

He *is* strong. Much stronger than you. Which means when there's a fight, you'll lose. And he *is* silent. Which means communication within the relationship is going to be a little strained and one-sided. Holding back information is actually one of his favourite pastimes. Mostly because it upsets you.

Well, what did you expect? Anyone described as 'dark' and 'brooding' is not going to be a naturally open, caring, sharing person. And Scorpio has a dark side that makes Darth Vader look like Mr Whippy. As for brooding ability, he leaves Heathcliffe out on the moors: he'll hold a grudge against you until the day you die. And your death will only appease him a little.

However, you'll never even know he has a grudge against you. A Scorpio bastard won't confront you openly. That would be too much like fair play. He's more likely to watch and wait – decades if necessary – for the chance to launch an attack when you're not paying attention. And when it finally hits, it'll make a stealth bomber look weak and clumsy.

Unfortunately, because of the amount of literature (if books featuring Fabio on the cover count as literature) you've absorbed, you'll class all his behaviour as normal. You'll revel in all the angst. Being miserable all the time must mean it's true love. This is all so romantic. You'll even be flattered by his possessiveness (despite the fact you're not allowed to go anywhere or see anyone). It means he can't bear to be without you. Of course, he can't bear to be with you either – not when there are still so many things wrong with you.

He'll manipulate you until you become exactly what he wants

you to be. Then he'll lose respect for you as you're so easily manipulated. Then he'll start looking around for someone else to manipulate. This is when you should start looking around too. For reputable psychiatric help. Because, in the midst of torturing you, Scorpio will suddenly turn into a model of gentleness and consideration. He'll even be kind to animals (standard behaviour for all romantic hero types – designed to suck you into believing they have a soft, sensitive side). Don't be fooled. It's just part of the callous game he's playing with your mental and emotional health. His objective is to annihilate you. But if he can make you believe he is incapable of such an act, it makes it so much more fun when he actually does destroy you.

And destroy you he will. This is what Scorpio does best. And besides, it's how he likes to spend his spare time. Once you are a broken mess on the floor he'll pick you up and glue you back together so you're whole once more and he can start all over again.

He takes his hobby very seriously. It brings him hours of enjoyment and allows him to explore his destructive talents. And you'll get something out of it too. A hobby of your own; a lifelong obsession with him. Which allows you to spend your spare time in expensive 12-step programmes undergoing extensive counselling.

Check into group therapy when you find yourself getting upset just because he is sleeping with other women. It's really none of your business. You *are* only his wife/girlfriend/mother of his children. And anyway, you'll meet his mistress soon enough when she joins the group after she discovers he's doing the same thing to her. Then you can console each other about your mutual stupidity. You'll both be introduced to a nationwide Unhealthily Obsessed Co-dependent Support Network for Women who have

Dated Scorpio. It comes complete with a 24-hour hotline, which you'll put to very good use. (This is a free-of-charge service, one of many sponsored by the Aspiring Romantic Novelists Association who use it for research purposes.)

The reason Scorpio inspires such obsessive behaviour is because he is so obsessive himself – about sex. He thinks about it twice as much as other men, which basically means it's on his mind all the time. Which makes him the blueprint for the complete and utter bastard. Which in turn makes women think he's sexy. Which therefore means he really can't help but catch one or two of the airborne little-black-dress-clad oestrogen packages continually throwing themselves his way. (Warning: don't be tempted to have an affair yourself to get back at your Scorpio bastard. Right now, you're in no emotional state to witness a jealous streak the size of the San Andreas fault. This is probably unnecessary advice as you won't have time between those ever-increasing therapy sessions and that compulsive shopping habit you recently developed. And, let's face it, the nervous twitch and chronic alcoholism aren't exactly going to be attracting men in droves.)

If it helps your sanity, blame the other poor, obsessed women. Or their therapists. Or the government. Or, better yet, blame yourself. No one forced you to read all those ridiculous love stories. You wanted a club-wielding, hair-dragging, heroic bastard. You've got him. Now you have to live with him. So, just throw yourself into his arms or under the next passing truck. Either way the ending will be the same.

HOW TO SPOT ONE

When a Scorpio bastard looks at you, you will feel a strong urge to shed your underwear. He will have this baffling effect upon you even if you're in a very public place and you find him most unattractive.

WHERE TO FIND ONE
Follow the trail of emotional wrecks to his door. Or, better still, let him find you. Because then, at least, you won't be the one who started the relationship which ruined your life.

HOW TO INTRIGUE ONE
Be sunny and happy and full of life. He won't be able to resist the challenge of luring you to the pits of hell. Once there, just be whatever he wants you to be. Holding on to your personality will only cause you a lot of unnecessary pain.

THE FIRST DATE
Scorpio will charm you into submission. Or else he'll worm his way into your life and affections without you noticing – like cancer or some other terminal disease. And after just one date, he'll know everything there is to know about you and you'll know absolutely nothing about him. This sets the tone for the entire relationship.

WHEN TO DO THE DEED
Because Scorpio has so many hidden agendas, you'll never be able to pick the right time. So go to bed when he wants to, generally just after you've been introduced. *(Tip: When you do it, make like a porn star but somehow give the impression you've never done it before.)*

WHEN TO POP THE QUESTION
If you feel the inclination to do this, have yourself committed.

IF HE DROPS YOU
Trying to exact revenge will only serve to amuse Scorpio as your attempts will seem so amateur. Besides, he'll be flattered he still has total control over your emotions and your life. On the other hand, running after him doing your best impersonation of a doormat will only invite him to clean his boots on you. Don't waste your energy. You'll need it over the next few years just to get through therapy.

IF YOU DROP HIM
He'll get over it. If, however, he thinks you've slighted him, it's best to watch out for yourself and take extra precuations for the next ten or 20 years. At least.

The Pisces Bastard

20 FEBRUARY–20 MARCH

To put it mildly, Pisces is a pathological liar. If you don't believe us, try this little quiz:

1. The Pisces bastard you love refuses to look you straight in the eye when he answers a slightly tricky question.

Right-aligned: *True/False?*

How to Spot a B*st*rd by his Star Sign

2. *He tries to avoid answering tricky questions whenever humanly possible.*

True/False?

3. *He says he loves you madly and has done at least one thing to prove it.*

True/False?

If you answered True to any of the above you are not dating a Pisces bastard. Either that or you are a Pisces bastard, and you're doing this quiz just to prove us right.

Because he's at the arse-end of the zodiac, Pisces is often referred to as the astrological 'rubbish tip'. What this means is he has a little bit of all the other star sign bastards in him which therefore makes him a bastard 12 times over. This in turn means he's obliged to tell massive fibs so you won't find out the awful truth.

When we first meet someone we like, it's only natural to pretend to be something we're not. Otherwise none of us would ever get a date. However, it's to what extent the truth is stretched that separates the rest of the world from Pisces. For instance, you might be a bus conductor but pretend you actually drive the bus. This is called a 'gross exaggeration'. Pisces, however, will be the bus driver and pretend it's a really interesting job. This is called an 'appalling lie'.

The lies he tells to make himself look better are not to be confused with the little white ones he tells to *protect your feelings* (although how he can confuse his arse with your feelings is a complete mystery to us).

When you accuse him of buying a house with his ex-girlfriend, he will deny it – even though you're holding the deeds embossed with his 'n' hers names. Instead he will say the real estate agent must have made a typing error. When you look at him in utter disbelief he'll say, okay then, he bought it by accident. When you fall about laughing maniacally, he'll whine that it wasn't his fault – it was yours – and, besides, she made him do it.

But it's the pointless fibs he tells which will really have you reaching for a gun. Pisces will tell you he watched an art house film when what he really did was sleep through it. He'll say he had a chicken and salad sandwich when he actually had a ham and salad sandwich. Why? Who the hell knows? We're not psychologists. Go ask his.

Fortunately, whilst Pisces was blessed with natural-born cunning and deceit, God denied him long-term vision. So even though he can lie through his teeth to his little heart's content, he won't have the foresight to remember what he said he did, who he said he did it to and why he did it to her in the first place. This means you will *always* find him out.

Obviously, the quicker off the mark you are, the sooner you'll spot the yawning chasm between fact and fiction and the faster you can drop him. Because, to be honest, once the initial thrill of catching him out wears off, you'll begin to resent being a full-time lie-detector on legs.

It goes without saying, Pisces only lies when he opens his mouth. This is why he isn't normally talkative. He figures if he doesn't talk, he can't lie – thus saving you and him a lot of unnecessary grief.

His impressive evasive techniques aren't limited to verbal

exchanges however. He also figures if he avoids you on a physical level, you won't see him for the truly gutless wonder he is.

Unfortunately this means he'll never be there for you when you actually do have need of him. Don't be upset when he misses the birth of your first child. He'll either have been waylaid because he forgot to put petrol in the car (and petrol is a real and tangible thing whereby he is not), or he's deliberately avoiding it because you might leave him holding the baby.

He's a loser. So why don't you kill him? Well, there's the mandatory life sentence to consider. And there's the community outrage to take into account – after all, everybody loves a Pisces bastard. He's so bloody nice and kind, he makes Mother Theresa want to throw up. Naturally, you end up looking like Lucrezia Borgia on a bad hair day whilst he's busy perfecting his saint *in situ* look.

Truth be known though, Pisces spends so much time thinking about how caring and sharing he is, he rarely has time to act upon it. That's why he *is* so sweet and tolerant. He never criticises your own foibles because if he does you can do likewise back to him (which you'll do anyway just so you can perpetuate the myth about how he's the second coming and you're a complete cow).

Let's be honest here, his passive-aggressive ways could test the patience of Gandhi. The innate ability of Pisces to sit and do and say nothing for years at a time means all decisions are made for him. By you. Which he secretly loves. Especially as most of them are to his detriment (i.e. you leave him) and he's such a consummate martyr. How else can he feel legitimately sorry for himself and get everyone else to do likewise?

'Everyone else' is all his ex-wives and ex-girlfriends, whom he hasn't quite let go because he hates to get rid of the past. Take the 'pack' out of 'packrat' and it's Pisces. He'll keep some of the polaroids, most of the love letters and all of the bits of fluff. Real astrologers misconstrue this as his intensely romantic nature. Unless we're missing something here, we're obliged to say it's obviously all inside his head. Don't expect to be deluged with expensive flowers, perfume or engagement rings unless he's just told a whopper and you've just found out. Sweet nothings are all you'll get.

With a straight face and without missing a beat (yes, we've learnt from the best), we can honestly say it's not *surprising* Pisces is known as the zodiac's biggest heartbreaker. Indeed, self-help books abound to help you try to get over him. Here's one for starters:

Lie back in your chair. Take a deep breath and count to ten. You are now feeling calmer – so imagine you're still in love with Pisces . . . Now bloody well wake up.

–Excerpt from *Dropping Pathetic Bastards Using Hypnotherapy* © Lang and Rajah 1998

HOW TO SPOT ONE

Your typical Pisces bastard often has light blue or green eyes. This is God's small way of helping you to spot pupil dilation more easily when he's telling a bald-faced lie. He'll also have small hands and feet – you will later note these are in direct proportion to his spine, brain and everything else that matters.

How to Spot a B*st*rd by his Star Sign

WHERE TO FIND ONE

On a cross feeling sorry for himself. In a Buddhist monastery attempting to stay celibate. At a cosmetic surgery at regular intervals having his nose reduced.

HOW TO INTRIGUE ONE

Take drugs, screw around and behave badly in public. Then blame it all on your sad, truly pathetic upbringing. This will make him feel better about his own shortcomings whilst at the same time make him want to save you in the vain hope you will look up to him for the rest of your life.

THE FIRST DATE

If you must go anywhere decent, organise it yourself. Otherwise you'll end up walking for miles looking for this really excellent Indian restaurant he's been to and knows is somewhere. Round the corner.

WHEN TO DO THE DEED

When he's drunk. When his girlfriend isn't looking. When he feels like it. Don't be surprised when you get had up for date rape in the morning if he regrets what he's done (i.e. if his girlfriend finds out).

WHEN TO POP THE QUESTION

Don't. Whilst your average Pisces bastard quite likes the idea of love ever after he isn't equipped to deal with harsh realities like showing up at the chapel on time, swearing on the Bible and saying 'I do' when he patently never does.

Water Signs

IF HE DROPS YOU

He won't as this would mean he'd have to be responsible for his own actions. Instead he'll engineer it so you have to do it for him – that is, he'll act so unavailable you'll be convinced you aren't going out with him anymore so therefore it's okay if you bonk someone else. This affords him the right to be duly devastated and root all his old flames in an attempt to get on with his life.

IF YOU DROP HIM

You'll play right into his martyr complex. In a cloud of self-denial, he'll start spending quality time with you by following you around in an unmarked car; he'll actually initiate phone calls for the first time ever (but hang up when you answer); and he'll take daring risks for once in his life by appearing at your apartment balcony without use of lift or stairs. The only thing to do is tell him you love him, all is forgiven and you'd like to be the mother of his children. You won't see him for dust. Trust us.

Which Bastard for which Goddess?

There are 12 beautiful, intelligent and charming star signs in the zodiac. All of them are women. And all of them, coincidentally, are reading this book. Including you.

As well as possessing the kind of looks that leave male stiffs strewn in your wake, the sort of genius that gives Stephen Hawkin an inferiority complex and the type of personality that makes fat, jolly people ashamed, you are also kind to small yappy dogs, charitable to Born-Again Christians and extremely patient with public servants. You are a true goddess and destiny will hand you the man of your dreams on a plate.

There is, unfortunately, not a lot you can do with just his head. Save kick it around or put it away in the third drawer in your kitchen, along with all the other useless junk you've accumulated during your lifetime. Best you send him straight back into the hands of the gods because you've got more chance of getting the peace, love and respect you deserve from the very nice bone china plate he came presented on.

You did *read* the last 12 chapters, didn't you? They're all *bastards*, remember? And you're destined to a life of true misery if you take up with any one of them (if you don't believe us, take a look at your mother's love life to date).

Don't be reassured by real astrologers. They're forced to prey on your foolish hopes; otherwise they lose valuable book advances, humungous commissions from 0891 lines, and an awful lot of well-heeled, often royal, private clients.

But not us two novice stargazers. We're going to tell it how it is, just so you don't get any ideas like, 'Oh, well, yes, I *know* Pisces is meant to piss off Leo and Sagittarius girls in a major way, but I'm a Cancer girl. And everybody *knows* Pisces boys and Cancer girls are *ever-so* compatible.'

The Aries Goddess

21 MARCH–20 APRIL

Being the strong, assertive sort, you can whip any one of the 12 miserable bastards into a blubbering mess in no time. Work your way up through Darwin's theory of natural selection and pick on the weakest one first.

When you do manage to track down Pisces at the chiropractor's, turn him into a gibbering wreck by telling him he's a 'spineless-good-for-nothing-who-couldn't-lie-straight-in-bed'. When he so much as dares to answer you back, prove actions speak louder than words and hit below the belt – that way he'll never be the father of anyone's children and you'll be doing the world a really big favour.

Proceed to storm into the adjoining beauty salon and teach 'dumb-brain-up-himself-for-no-good-reason' Libra that there's no such thing as a fair fight and knee him in the groin when he's not looking in the mirror.

In the next room, 'he's-got-no-idea-but-you-can't-have-it-all-especially-if-you're-Virgo', Virgo is having his routine colonic irrigation treatment. When he correctly points out you kneed Libra in the groin the wrong way and, here, he'll show you how to do it properly, make him understand who's doing what wrong and give him a good kick up the backside.

'He's-so-oblivious-he-won't-know-what's-hit-him' Aquarius won't notice all the bodies writhing around in agony when he wanders on in for his weekly scalp massage. Get his attention by head-butting him and then, after he moans on about having a severe brain haemorrhage, toss him an Aspro.

Start feeling sorry for all these losers but soon decide to get a grip. So grab hold of 'unthinking-unattractive-un-everything' Sagittarius and begin to throttle him.

Feel that unfamiliar nagging sense of guilt again and decide against your own strong will to get some counselling. In the waiting-room order 'jumped-up-jelly-brained' Gemini to shut up or else. When he just simply can't, show him one of your own rather scary sides and tongue-lash him to death.

After the shrink says you're too soft for your own good, take his advice and throw yourself into a self-assertiveness training camp out in the country. There in a paddock, lead bull-headed

How to Spot a B*st*rd by his Star Sign

Taurus around by the nose whilst complaining 'he's-always-following-me-and-why-doesn't-he-get-a-life-of-his-own-and-let-me-get-on-with-mine?' When he just doesn't get it, wound him with well-chosen words like 'fat', 'lazy' and 'useless' and deliberately leave the gate open.

Notice 'completely-unnoticeable-except-when-I-trip-over-your-wallet' Capricorn outside the gate diligently flogging logs to unseeing passers-by and tell him 'he's-a-disgusting-old-goat-who'll-only-get-to-the-top-of-the-corporate-ladder-because-every one-else-has-run-fleeing-from-it'.

Hear 'his-head's-too-big-for-his-you-know-what' Leo laughing at your rapier-like wit whilst gazing fondly at his full head of hair in the reflection on the nearby pond. Turn your attention to him and laugh at him too. As he skulks off in wounded pride, put the boot in by telling him 'you're-not-that-big-anyway-and-I-was-only-faking-it-so-there'.

At this point 'he-gives-me-the-creeps-but-someone's-got-to-be-nice-to-him-because-he's-got-no-friends' Cancer crawls out from the pond and sidles up to you. Regress to your old bad habits and kick him really hard. When he still refuses to let go of your foot, shake him off by saying 'mummy's-expecting-you-home-for-dinner-so-scat'.

Then spot 'if-that's-what-qualifies-as-sex-on-a-stick-I'll-skip-the-icy-pole-thanks' Scorpio lounging in the dirt looking tall, dark and something. Confuse him by refusing to play mind games. Suggest an arm-wrestle instead and twist *his* around his back and force him to list his faults. Get bored with listening to them all and shove him into a ditch.

After all these exhausting courtships and what seems like a totally fruitless weekend, decide men are 'a-bunch-of-sad-no-hoper-weaklings-and-where's-the-bloody-challenge?'

'Over here,' says 'too-big-for-his-boots-too-small-for-his-trousers' Aries. Go ahead, make your day. Deny his greatness whilst at the same time taking care to emphasise your own. That should piss him off, well and truly. Good, The trip hasn't been wasted after all.

The Taurus Goddess

21 April–21 May

When it comes to dogged perseverance and unswerving faith in mankind, thinly disguised as sheer stupidity, you truly have no peers.

After Aries tells you he genuinely believes in commitment, you genuinely believe him and start designing your wedding dress. When he goes on to say he believes in commitment so much that he can't leave his wife (particularly since she owns and runs his business) you procure a good lawyer on his behalf.

Then, when he still can't bring himself to make an honest woman of you as he's got to wait for his kids to leave/be expelled from school, Aquarius asks why you're seeing a married man who has no intention of marrying you. You tell him to curl up and die because his opinions don't count. Upon which, upon reflection, he feels forced to agree.

Cancer enters the fray and leaves soon after because he thinks you haven't noticed him yet. But, out of the corner of your eye, you've already registered his peculiar sidewards gait and it appeals to your charitable nature. You ask him if he needs help, he mutters something unprintable and you do something unmentionable. Like kiss him.

Of course, Virgo is totally repulsed by all the bodily contact he's just witnessed but, as usual, can't bring himself to do anything about it. You try valiantly to arouse him into action and put your back out in the process.

Even you eventually get sick of his perpetual low-achieving ways and set your sights on the far more gung-ho Capricorn. Be dazzled by his gold AMEX card but stubbornly refuse to see that most of his long hours at the office are done with a blonde, blue-eyed assistant called Deb-short-for-Debutante who, following your example, always bends over backwards for him.

Leo is only too happy to be taken on the rebound as you haven't told him you're actually on it. But in the long run you get tired of his constant bragging. When he starts blubbing and says he only does it because he's so insecure, you endeavour to help him become more self-confident which, since he's already such a bighead, only serves to make him more obnoxious.

Suddenly, the Pisces who won't look you in the eye because he's so shy/dishonest, starts to look mildly appealing. You rally round, find him a house to live in, a career to excel at and a backbone to be proud of – but to no avail. When the pressure gets too much he tippy-toes out of your life and back to his old girlfriend whilst you're busy reading *How To Rein In Another Commitment-Phobe Before He Actually Bolts*.

Naturally, you then seek solace in a fellow Taurus who in turn seeks comfort in food. You tell him you'd love to join him but your metabolism is lower, your fat cell content higher and if you too looked like a gross pig he would never have fancied you in the first place.

Which is why you're silly enough to fall for Scorpio. With him you burn off kilojoules you haven't yet consumed. Unfortunately, he takes pleasure in wrecking all the good sex work-outs you've just done by squeezing your naked thighs in broad daylight.

Esteem in tatters, you book in for extensive liposuction and share a ward with Libra who's actually booked in for brain surgery but thought he'd have a bit of a nip and tuck whilst he's at it. His good looks – despite the bruising under the eyes and the stitches around his forehead – impress you but his dilly-dallying over whether to have his cornflakes with or without milk sorely tests your patience.

It therefore follows that your slightly scatty Sagittarius surgeon inspires no confidence whatsoever. No matter how many times you try to reassure him, his hands still shake when he holds the scalpel, the biro he's supposed to mark the incisions with has just run out and you don't see why you have to take your bra off when he's only meant to be sucking cellulite from your legs.

When you do eventually come out of the anaesthetic, you think you're seeing double but it's just the Gemini orderly attracted by your single-minded ways. However, you are completely alarmed by his lack thereof. Trying to organise his complex life is way too hard and after you've tried plan A, try plan B and check out of hospital.

Eventually come to the conclusion your love life has turned into a bit of a sheltered workshop – except this lot couldn't put a stamp on an envelope unless you licked one first and told them where to stick it.

The Gemini Goddess

Blessed with a chameleon-like nature and an ability to fall in and out of love in a matter of seconds, you believe yourself capable of being all things to all men all at once. So why waste yourself on just one? Our sentiments exactly.

Become a femme fatale for Aries. He won't know how to deal with a level of sophistication so far above his own. Use big words when answering his grunts and remain conscious during sex. He'll be so confused he'll think he's in love and offer to mate with you for life. Leave him before he has a chance to make good his offer.

Act like an innocent so that Scorpio appears. He'll be suspicious of a 32-year-old virgin and will want to investigate further. Then while virtuously maintaining you have no practical knowledge of sex, accidentally put yourself through every position in the *Kama Sutra*. Afterwards, light a cigarette, yawn and tell him if that's what sex is all about you don't know why you even bothered. Then duck.

Transform yourself into a clinging vine and sleep with Sagittarius. Wake up the next morning, tell him you love him and ask when he's going to marry you. Now see how long it takes him to get to the next county. If you've nothing better to do, follow him to the next county and see how long it takes to make him leave the country.

Come back as the very young wife (and sole heir) of a very

old, very rich man who, unfortunately, has a very weak heart. Explain to Capricorn your husband's doctors don't expect him to live the week and ask him nicely if he can lend you the £5,000 you'll need until then (as you really don't want to bother hubby while he's attached to the life-support system). Capricorn will figure he'll get a good return on his investment and hand it over. Take the money and run.

Then act as though you have a conscience, look for Aquarius and sit up all night discussing the morality of your actions. In return for him listening to you talk non-stop for seven or eight hours, allow him to lecture you on the ethical downfalls of taking advantage of another human being. But as soon as the shops open in the morning point out that Capricorn is hardly human and indulge in a guilt-free spending spree.

Buy yourself a pair of those expensive designer mirrored sunglasses and find Leo gazing deeply into your eyes. Tell him you think as highly of him as he does and watch him shower you with flowers and chocolates. Keep flattering him and he'll beg you to make him the happiest man on earth. Let him know you wouldn't if he were the last man on earth.

Turn to Taurus, feed the chocolates to him, and convince him all you really want is to settle down and raise a family. Wait the hour or so it takes for all this information to sink in and be rewarded by him making a slow lunge in your general direction.

After rejecting Taurus as he was uncivilised enough to propose to you with his mouth full, be yourself and make Pisces fall in love with you. It should take only a matter of minutes. To ensure he stays in love with you forever dump him immediately and remember to use uncalled-for cruelty.

Leave him in peace to enjoy his self-pity and turn on all your charm for Virgo who, sadly, has none. Fake a genuine interest in his match-book collection and request that he starts one for you – beginning with matches from a quaint little bar you know in Greenland.

Assure him you'll wait in chastity for his return (to continue the rest of your lives together – also in chastity) and whilst he's gone go bonk Libra and fall hopelessly in love for the five minutes the sex lasts. See how shallow you both can be together and realise he has you beaten. Decide to leave (as he can't).

Make like you have maternal instincts (it's okay, no one who knows you will believe it) and bump into Cancer. Try to talk yourself into liking him even though nobody else does. Give up after a concerted two-minute effort. Then decide to call his mother and tell her you are concerned about him.

Change your mind and call up fellow Gemini instead. Arrange a time and place to meet so you can both forget and stand each other up. Forget you have stood him up and call him up again – after a few calls the relationship will be too emotionally demanding for either of you. So drop it, because by now you won't be able to remember any of your dating experiences with the other bastards so you can start all over again.

The Cancer Goddess

22 June–23 July

Your natural, nurturing instinct means you have to beat the bastards off with a broom. They all crawl out of your freshly veneered woodwork hoping to spend the rest of their crummy lives in domestic bliss, unaware you only look after those you massively love – let alone actively dislike.

Taurus is first in line, doggy-bag in hand. Put him off by showing your fridge (the one with the false bottom). The real one features one bottle of really bad cooking sherry and a shrunken lemon. For the *pièce de résistance*, open the freezer so he can see the human corpse inside.

Once Taurus has run off into the night (and we use the verb 'run' very loosely here) let Virgo thaw out, because he wants to live forever and you can't think for a moment why.

Aquarius materialises from behind your blender and says he can think for a moment why. You let him talk himself stupid because he is and, besides, it gives you the vital 30 seconds you need to whip up that boil-in-the-bag gourmet meal-for-one.

When Aries lurches in and proclaims processed foods are bad for you and all you need is the love of a good man who can buy you a proper wood stove, you momentarily fall for his pick-up line but are soon put off when he insists you take off your shoes to make love over the kitchen sink.

You next nip Cancer's cheap carnations and smug aspirations in the bud by slamming the door in his face. He might feel home is where the heart is, but he's got the bloody wrong address.

As that one sulks off into the night, another one slithers in. It's Scorpio with all the accoutrements – bottle of wine, dark chocolates, love letter his wife once wrote him, and a bulk-pack of condoms. Take the wine (it's a good vintage), take the chocolates (that's dinner for three nights) and bin his purported prose. As for the condoms – well, you're far too much of a lady to comment though, suffice it to say, they make very good rubber gloves for small dainty hands if you sew five of them together.

Distracted by your pattern cutting you make the mistake of letting filthy, grotty Sagittarius into the house. He leaves damp sheets everywhere, tries to mate with your next-door neighbour's teenage daughter and makes you cry with thoughtless comments like, 'there's no way I'm going to meet all your inbred relatives'.

Naturally, after him, seasoned charmer Libra seems like a breath of fresh air. Until you realise you can't manacle air, make it commit and compel it to have your babies.

Now terrified of ending up an old maid, you allow Pisces to sneak into the house. He won't propose to you either but at least he'll make you realise relationships aren't everything. And, since he spends most of his time avoiding the issue by crawling under the house looking for excuses or up in the loft in search of the truth, it's easy for you to conduct an illicit affair with the sexy beast who's seconded the settee downstairs.

Unfortunately, whilst you *are* in a passionate clinch with Leo, you can't help but hear the clink of coins. You are duly stunned when your current inamorato stomps off in disgust because you stopped rolling your eyes to the back of your head for a split milli-second.

The culprit, Capricorn, is bottling all the money he's retrieved from under the cushions on your couch. But, no matter how attractive his bank account is, even you find it hard to put up with such a humourless drone. He's neat and clean around the house but so is household cleaner. And at least the household cleaner comes with a money-back guarantee.

It stands to reason you soon become enamoured with fun-loving Gemini who's talking to Basil and Rosemary in the pots on your window-sill. However, his inability to stand still long enough to wait for dinner to be cooked – in a microwave – ends up frazzling your nerves.

As you survey the debris, the crumbs and the stains on the carpet, you come to the conclusion that looking after men and keeping the house nice is not what it's cracked up to be. As tears trickle down your apron you resolutely cancel your subscription to *Family Circle* and get a life instead.

The Leo Goddess

24 JULY–23 AUGUST

No man is truly worthy of your astrological royalty. But since these peasants are forever hurling themselves at your imperial feet, you'll get tired of stepping over them. So if you must consort with the masses, it's best to begin with something light.

The first fool to rush in is Sagittarius – but we said light, not completely weightless, so try four to five years with a nice, noncommital Libra instead. He'll be happy to be with you until the next, younger and more beautiful princess comes along. Then he'll be happy to be with her.

Once you get back to court, you'll discover there's very little left to arrange to marry. Don't despair. Your prince will come. Enter Scorpio, heir to the throne of Transylvania and a very good reason to leave the room.

As you go, one of those slow, plodding Taurus types follows at a respectful distance. Test this simpleton's loyalty: let him eat cake or spend time with you. (To make this fair, use a triple chocolate cake covered in Lindt balls.) Then get out of the way as he dives for the cake.

Dust off the crumbs and notice Pisces flopping at your feet, opening and closing his mouth, emitting I'm-not-worthy noises. Listen to him, he's actually telling the truth – for the first time in his life.

As soon as you've retired to your ivory tower to let your hair down, Gemini calls to you, promising to build you a castle in the air. But once you're as firmly ensconced as you can be in a virtual building you won't be amused by his lack of attention. Just walk out when he's looking the other way. It'll take him years to work out exactly what is missing from his life.

As you make good your escape, you trip over Cancer as he pathetically attempts to be a human carpet for you. Kick him. This will turn the carpet red – as it should be.

Now you cancel all public appearances and take yourself into seclusion. Here you find Aquarius trying to find himself. Unfortunately (for him), he believes in treating all people, royalty or otherwise, the same. As well as this obvious disrespect, he has an annoying habit of disappearing without taking his leave of you. Don't waste a search party on him; use a creep-seeking missile instead.

Romance hasn't worked for you thus far so try a logical, sensible choice of partner to please your adoring public. You briefly try the crown on Capricorn, a man with such a sound financial head it seems a waste to cut it off. However, this is the penalty for giving unsolicited stock-market forecasts on the hour every hour.

And, as Virgo will tell you – over and over again – the law is the law. Use the law, the one about stating the bloody obvious, to banish this boring subject from the kingdom and take away his discount phonecard to avoid ever having to listen to him again.

We have now changed our royal mind about romance and are willing to give it another try. So the two guys clanking around in the corner, busily applying Silvo to their armour and admiring their reflections, will turn your head. Aries waves his – um – lance in the air and tells you to look no further than his rugged self. You can't as the sun has glinted off the spoilers on his armour, half-blinding you.

In desperation you knight the remaining Leo. Unfortunately, during the ceremony the sword slips, pricking and deflating his ego (it wasn't your fault, it was so big it got in the way).

Now all your suitors have been tried and found wanting, realise just how much fun it is to be the queen, deciding the fate of the common man. Appoint Gemini court jester, put Capricorn in charge of the treasury, make Virgo head of grape-peeling and have the rest thrown in the dungeon. But make sure Pisces and Scorpio get fed properly. You'll probably want to take them out now and then for sex.

The Virgo Goddess

24 August–23 September

Look, we understand that relationships are hard things to keep tidy and men just naturally seem to have so many faults. But you'll just have to consider this your duty (and you are never one to shirk duty). We'll try to make it as clean and efficient as possible. Just arrange yourself on your crisp cotton sheets and wait for love to appear. We have arranged appointments for all 12 bastards and they should be arriving in an astrologically orderly manner.

8 a.m. Perhaps this one wasn't such a good one to start with. Yes, he is a trifle overpowering, isn't he? That's Aries for you. He is a bit barbaric. Well, yes, we can understand you don't want him moulting any body hair on your bed, but he really likes you. He says you are so feminine it makes him want to . . . no, he doesn't believe in trimming his nose hairs . . . okay then. Next . . .

9 a.m. Yes, Taurus. A very solid chap . . . No, he just asked if you were serving breakfast at this interview . . . Next . . .

10.25 a.m. This is Gemini. Yes, he is 25 minutes late. No, he doesn't seem to have an explanation. Yes, we think he should stand still and shut up too. No, he can't help flirting with all of us – it's his nature . . . Next . . .

11 a.m. Cancer. Such a vulnerable little soul. Yes, and such sad eyes. No, he doesn't get out much . . . No, he says he likes it when you criticise him, it reminds him of his mother. Yes, that is perverted . . . Next . . .

12 noon. This is Leo. He says you've probably heard of him; he says he's quite famous. What's that you say? You've never heard of him in your life . . . No, you didn't say anything wrong at all – he's just kind of sensitive about stuff like that . . . Next . . .

12.55 p.m. Virgo is here. Yes, very punctual – early actually. Seems nice, you say? . . . Yes, he does get on your nerves after a while. No, no, you're not like him at all . . . Next . . .

2.10 p.m. Libra. He is nice and boyish looking. Why is he

standing over there? Well, it seems he can't make up his mind whether or not to come in. He likes the look of you but is frightened there might be a better girl conducting interviews today . . . yes, we think so to . . . Next . . .

3.15 p.m. This is Scorpio. No, he says he's late on purpose. No, as far as we know he doesn't have X-ray vision and he can't see through your nightdress. That's just the way he always looks at women. He says he's here because he heard you were a virgin . . . Well, he wasn't to know that . . . Next . . .

4.05 p.m. Yes, it's Sagittarius . . . look, he didn't mean to break that vase . . . or that one . . . No, he's not dangerous, just clumsy. We actually think you might like him once you . . . oh, was that another vase? . . . Next . . .

5 p.m. Capricorn, right on time. Now here's someone you can relate to – he's practical and good with money. And he thinks you're just about perfect. Is he romantic? . . . er . . . Next . . .

6–7 p.m. Yes, it was supposed to be Aquarius. No, we don't know why he didn't show either. Yes, it is probably for the best . . . Next . . .

8 p.m. Pisces. Yes, he is terribly sweet . . . and gentle . . . and romantic . . . He says you're the purest, sweetest thing he has ever seen. Yes, that is nice . . . no, he says stuff like that all the time but he never means a word of it . . . er, except, of course, in this case . . . No, we don't know where he's going either . . . No, we don't know if he's coming back . . .

That's all there is. You were right about them (you're always right), they aren't worth soiling your knickers over. You'll just have to continue being a paragon of virtue. No, you're not too fussy at all. But perhaps we should call it a day. After all, you have got to get back to the convent.

The Libra Goddess

24 SEPTEMBER–23 OCTOBER

You tend to give too much credence to bastards and their pathetic bastard excuses for their criminal bastard behaviour. You have to realise that giving them the benefit of the doubt is to give them yet another benefit they don't deserve. Remember this as you pass judgement on the 12 hard cases who are about to throw themselves at your mercy.

Pisces is the first law-breaker to be dragged squealing into court. Ask him where he was last night and he'll invent an alibi. Sentence him to five years hard labour for perjury. Or give him 30 lashes so he won't be able to lie comfortably in any position.

The next case is over before it begins. That Aries thug has committed too many offences against you and your gender to be given much of a hearing – the worst offence being his inability to differentiate between a common greeting and foreplay. Lock him up. Then lock up the key.

Sagittarius, the racketeer and bane of his probation officer's life, will upset any order in your court. Set bail at £50,000. He'll never have that kind of money (or any, come to think of it) so he won't be able to practise his bad habit of skipping the country whenever things go wrong in a relationship.

Now you'll encounter a wrongdoer who stubbornly refuses to admit his guilt; he was right, the rest of the world was wrong. Tell Taurus you haaf vaays of making him talk and charge him for crimes against humanity.

Then convict Gemini for fraudulently impersonating someone with a heart and double his sentence when he tries to tell you he can't go to jail as he's only a minor *(see chapter on The Gemini Bastard)*. But let him off when he finally pleads insanity and put him away in a nice, comfortably padded cell somewhere.

Cancer now takes the stand and claims he was abused as a child, hoping this excuse will stand up for himself – as he can't – and if it doesn't, well, he has a note from mother. Because you know he secretly craves punishment let him off on a good behaviour bond and place him back under the protective care of you-know-who. Then take a short recess when he starts to cry.

When court is once more in session you'll meet a smooth-talking gangster who thinks he can charm you out of all your convictions. Leo believes he is above the law and expects you to turn a blind eye to his nocturnal activities.

You'll be grateful Leo is roaring in outrage at your decision to ignore him as it drowns out Virgo trying to state his own case. He prides himself on being a textbook criminal, so he'll read the entire thing to you. You'll have to throw the book at him because he can't be allowed to remain at large in society. People might have to talk to him.

Libra is a threat to no one but himself. So treat him as merely an accessory to a minor crime and give him a light sentence to match his personality.

Go from petty to unspeakable crime as you question Scorpio and glimpse the underworld. Let him go. He's definitely guilty but you're powerless to stop corruption this great. Anyway, justice will be served, criminals of his level tend to be found sooner or later wearing concrete flippers at the bottom of a river.

After this brush with gangland, Aquarius seems a simple punk with a penchant for breaking rules – give him a law to live by and he'll try to break it on principle. So tell him it's a crime to be so annoying and take away the freedom he yearns for. And when he cries 'unfair', gently let him know that life is unfair, so tough shit.

Turn to Capricorn and white-collar crime at its best. He managed to rob your bank account without even getting his hands dirty and now expects the state to support him if convicted. As he's the last case, make an example of him – bring back hanging as the punishment for money-grabbing social climbers.

In the future, keep your reputation as the judge of dread. It may limit your love life to a certain degree but it'll also make the bastards behave themselves a little better in your presence. But remember: they're all guilty until proven innocent.

The Scorpio Goddess

24 OCTOBER–22 NOVEMBER

Realising that women everywhere are counting on you to give all bastards the untold misery, mayhem and plagues of sexually transmitted diseases they truly deserve, you plot and scheme your way through the entire zodiac without getting out of bed for less than 10,000 spermatozoa a day.

First, emasculate Aries by turning the battle of the sexes into the battle of the exes. Sleep with all of his friends. Because you're no longer bothering to feign orgasms for him, he accuses you of having an affair and threatens to beat your lover to a pulp. You coolly ask 'which one?'.

Go on to punish Taurus by whipping out your rubber and beating him half to death. When he still stubbornly refuses to admit he's a dud in bed, teach him a lesson by tying his thickset limbs to the bedposts with industrial-strength pantyhose. Then leave him there.

Next, send Gemini to the nuthouse from whence he should have come by deliberately playing with the personalities inside his head. Tell Zoltan the unemployed, thick-as-a-brick construction worker, that Walter the neurotic middle-aged bundle-of-nerves, has the hots for him. Casually mention to Mikey, the shy, frightened child within, that Walter's got designs on him. Then have a small chat with Charles, the latent homosexual lawyer who's in love with Walter and also happens to be Mikey's father. Let drop to him that Zoltan's having an affair with Walter but really fancies Mikey.

Flushed with your success so far, decide it's high time Leo's confidence in himself was completely undermined. Mutter, 'I think you're brilliant, truly', whilst walking backwards to the nearest fire exit, gathering your black silk lingerie as you go. When he just doesn't get it (because he thinks you mean everything you say, especially the nice bits) spell it out to him – Y.O.U. A.R.E. C.R.A.P. I.N. B.E.D.

Be kind to be cruel to Cancer by sleeping with him. Then be nice to his mother to the point where she likes you more than him. When he stamps his foot and demands his teddy bear back, give it to him. Minus its head.

Then wheel Virgo into the bedroom and lure him into doing

things he's never dreamt of doing, like having rampant missionary position sex. When he becomes a fully-fledged member of the human race, decide you like him better when he wasn't one and put him back into his iron lung.

After bonking his brains out, confuse Libra by telling him you don't think he's very good looking. Unbalance him a bit more by asking him his opinion on anything that doesn't concern himself. As he desperately reaches for an answer, reach for his bus fare home.

Play Scorpio at his own game and win overwhelmingly because you're a woman and he's a man. Refuse to have sex with him and run off with his wife instead.

Scare Sagittarius witless during a post-coital fag by going along with all his outrageous plans without so much as a smirk. Now he'll feel obliged to go through with that wacky one-man walk through the Sahara with neither sunscreen nor water bottle. At the last minute, beg off accompanying him using foolproof excuses like you think he's a complete and utter idiot.

Destroy Capricorn's *raison d'être* by putting an anonymous call through to the Taxation Department's investigation unit whilst he's in your bathroom struggling to put on his condom. When he's forced to back-pay undeclared interest (and not just from his bank statements) make his life easier by demonstrating how to put on a condom correctly. With your teeth.

End the age of Aquarius by demanding sex once a day. That should kill him. If, however, it doesn't, give him an aneurism by resorting to cheap tricks like dying your hair blonde, answering all his questions with 'yah', 'nah' or 'very' and reading Jackie Collins novels upside down.

Deceive Pisces by telling him you'll swallow anything. When

he tentatively asks if you're pulling his leg, tell him if that's his leg you're pulling then he must be a dwarf and an extremely small one at that.

Now they're all mere husks of men and five o'clock shadows of their former selves, what the hell are you going to do in the future for fun? Lure the bastards back for round two, that's what.

The Sagittarius Goddess

23 NOVEMBER–21 DECEMBER

Your fickle, flighty nature, together with the kind of optimism that should come with a white stick and a doctor's note, means you'll date just about anything with a prostate gland and a valid passport. This, of course, adds up to more than a few gouges on your portable bedpost.

Use them to horrify possessive, stay-at-home types like Taurus. As you're not a particularly adept liar, you'll feel compelled to spill the names, addresses and favourite flags of every one of your conquests. On your first date.

To cheer yourself up when he calls again, pick up one of those desperate Cancer things who always seem to be furtively lurking under famous bridges. Listening to his terminal gripes will be enough to make your own traumas seem positively uplifting.

Now you're back in high spirits, be true to your nature and do something to wilfully wreck it. Hook up with Capricorn who's in Amsterdam – on business. Your lively ways and innate sense of humour will be wasted on him (if he guffaws at the punchline then you'll just *know* you've told the joke wrong). So have a laugh at his expense by ditching him after you've hoovered the zeros out of his Swiss bank account.

Spend the money profligately in Belgium in front of Virgo who'll have a quiet fit because a noisy one will muss up his hair. In no time he'll be boring you absolutely rigid and be too thick to realise, even after you tactlessly tell him. To make him go away, resort to uncharacteristic malice like deliberately un-alphabetising his compact disc collection.

During the short dry spell that follows, fly to LA and have a meaningless fling with no-strings-attached Libra. When you get sick of his unbearable lightness of being, drive him away with intentional intenseness. Questions like 'Do you like me yet?' should do the trick.

Go from one extreme to another: go to Eastern Europe and get involved with deep and just plain mean Scorpio. Revel in the drama of it all for the 15 minutes it takes you to affect a foreign accent, pick up the Romanian equivalent of an Oscar and get paid £60,000 to reveal all in the *News of the World*.

At the same time, give Aquarius from another planet a quick once-over just to reassure yourself that whilst the two of you might make a very good match in another life, this one is far too short for you to waste precious seconds on someone who takes himself so seriously.

Be determinedly single for a couple of hours before moving to Las Vegas and falling deeply in self-love with a fellow Sagittarius. Then lay bets on who will cheat on whom first.

Decide you're the winner and leave him for Aries who's just

been chucked out of Africa. Indulge in some mutual blood-letting and be devastated when the insurance company ups your home contents premium – again. Suggest to Aries that maybe now is the time to invest in self-assembly furniture so it can be taken apart and put back together again with greater ease.

When he says, 'You don't know what you're talking about and where's dinner?' leg it to France and get involved in a hopeless love triangle with Leo and his ego. Threaten to tell his wife (about you, not the implant). Then threaten to leave. Then be forced on sheer principle to follow through when he shows you the door.

On your way out, notice Gemini gabbling to himselves outside the Tower of Babel in Babylon. Feel a real meeting of the minds until you realise you can't ever get a word in edgeways because he's always interrupting himself.

Proceed to throw yourself at the shifty-eyed Pisces who's cowering behind the armoured tanks in Tiananmen Square. Believe everything he says, even the bit about how his fingers are permanently crossed behind his back because they're arthritic. To while away the few minutes the relationship lasts, play 'Truth or Dare' and wonder why such a seemingly honest, fearless type like him can't do either. Come to your senses when it's all too late and have a quick nervous breakdown just for the hell of it.

Resolve in future to only date men who have the same strength of spirit and sense of adventure as yourself. Hear something about a mysterious new thirteenth star sign. Book a one-way ticket and decide to check it out.

The Capricorn Goddess

22 DECEMBER–20 JANUARY

You find men, at best, boring and unnecessary. But with a little application and a slight change in attitude you can have fun, fulfil your ambitions and satisfy your need for control by taking every single one of them for a ride.

Start small with Aries. Overlook the fact he still lives in the Stone Age and don't criticise the way he handles money. He doesn't understand currency. He still uses a bartering system, the 'Gimme that or I'll beat you up' form of exchange. Offer to take his bearskin coat to the dry-cleaner and he'll readily agree as he thinks laundry is a woman's job anyway. And by emptying his pockets each time, you'll end up with a tidy little sum to leave him with.

Unless you want to throw this money away steer clear of Gemini. He's always in the middle of making a deal and will try to talk you into backing him. And being the ultimate con artist, he stands a fair chance of sucking in someone even as financially astute as you. Just remember, he's better at picking pockets than you are.

Try to avoid Pisces as well. He has absolutely no money-making habits and is of no other practical use. But, in passing, take the time out to explain this to him and destroy one of his little fantasies (i.e. he can be a business success and make it in the real world) in the process.

Being basically good-hearted, you'll feel sorry for what you've done and marry Taurus as penance. He isn't at all exciting but he understands money so it's worth taking him for half of everything he's got. However, he does have a possessive streak where both you and money are concerned. But if you handle the whole thing quickly and efficiently he'll never catch on.

Side-step Cancer. He'll pretend he does his own banking but the truth is he still gets an allowance from mother. And what's in the piggy bank is not enough to make you want to put up with him. Take up with Libra instead. You'll see through him because there's not much to see through and he'll see you as someone he can ditch when someone better comes along. Sure he can, but it'll cost him. Let him know you're serious by re-enacting a scene from *Fatal Attraction*. His credit card will be yours before you're finished. (Unfortunately, there won't be a hell of a lot of credit on it as his bank manager trusts him even less than his girlfriends do.)

Don't waste your dramatic mood – set your sights on a self-exhibiting Leo. He's probably the antithesis of everything you believe in – but fame and fortune aren't as discriminating as you are. Riches and recognition are quite likely to plop themselves at his feet for no good reason. So ask for nothing more than to bask in his reflected glory until he finds it impossible to live without you – then ask for 50 per cent.

For a complete change of pace turn to Virgo and become business partners (well, what else would you want him for – even you aren't that mercenary). Get to work as it's the only thing you'll have in common, apart from your mutual dislike of sex with each other. Through your astute leadership and his eye for detail you'll amass a fortune in no time. Split the money down the middle and depart before he gets any ideas about the two of you becoming a permanent arrangement.

Then for pure life experience approach Scorpio, but do it carefully. There will be an almighty struggle for power which could go on endlessly. So tell him the only hard thing he has that you're interested in is his cash and watch him disappear into the darkness muttering something about revenge.

Ignore him and get on with working towards financial independence by tackling Sagittarius and Aquarius together. Neither of them are worth a go by themselves as chances are they won't ever amount to anything. But by doubling your chances you'll probably break even. Sagittarius could stumble on to wealth through sheer dumb luck. And Aquarius could (through no fault of his own) make a fortune as a side-effect of his quest to make the world a better place. And as neither of them are particularly materialistic . . . well, you know what they say about fools and money.

You have enough capital now to interest a fellow Capricorn. Together you can buy all the happiness you could possibly want. However, you'll get sick of hearing the two jokes he knows, so rather than wasting money buying him a new joke book, fight him for the joint fortune instead. And, because you're dealing with another professional, this time the winner takes all . . . Now you can retire in comfort.

The Aquarius Goddess

21 January–19 February

Your enviable ability to breeze through life living inside your head and outside of reality means you don't actually give any bastard so much as a second glance, let alone a second thought.

You honestly don't see Leo lolling on your single bed in a leopard-skin loincloth doing his own small, sad impression of a *Playgirl* centrefold. However, the smell of his cheap aftershave does manage to get up your nose.

After lighting a couple of joss sticks, you clamber into bed beside him, turn over and promptly fall out, straight into the arms of a panting, slathering Sagittarius who's lying prone on the floor in anticipation of the seductress he's convinced lies hidden inside you.

You absent-mindedly walk all over him on the way to the bathroom where you altogether miss Virgo crouching over the toilet bowl because he's making himself so sick.

As you turn on the shower, you sense a second presence but it's only Cancer scrubbing the tiles in a futile attempt to impress you. You leave him to his own devices because subconsciously you know it's better than letting him touch yours.

When you reach for a towel you don't care to notice someone staring at you from the vanity mirror. Whilst you *could* be doing your best impression of a simpering siren, he *will* be doing his best impression of a Libra. Mortified that you don't appreciate him for the sex god he has finally decided he is (especially after you bluntly tell him he isn't), he beats a hasty retreat declaring you're frigid to the bastard patiently waiting for the bathroom.

This, of course, makes Taurus rise to the challenge. He traipses after you, down the corridor, through the lounge room and into the kitchen. Here, you'll vaguely hear the fridge door opening by itself and will, no doubt, puzzle over the missing wheel of Camembert in the morning.

How to Spot a B*st*rd by his Star Sign

In the morning whilst you contemplate whisking up an omelette *sans* cheese, the lovelorn cries of Aries doing his best impersonation of Tarzan-the-Ape through the kitchen window passes completely over your head. He lands unmanly like on the dining table and is forced to share space with your cats.

The doorbell rings, and you think it's the phone. When you pick it up you hear a clot of heavy breathing and feel compelled to ask how the caller is and if there's anything you can do to cure his asthma. When he coughs, clears his throat and, ahem, explains he's Scorpio attempting to talk dirty, you launch into an in-depth monologue about the effect of iambic pentameter on the decline of the Western civilisation until he's forced to slam the phone down in total disgust.

The doorbell is still ringing so you accidentally open the door on your way to somewhere else you were going. There, you stand face to faces with another person who is not quite of this world. Gemini is hopping from one foot to another, different hats in hand, waiting to propose. You tell him that you're dreadfully sorry, but you don't give money to lost causes any more.

Capricorn then pops out from behind the bonsais and tells you that it's a really good tax deduction and jokingly asks if you've heard the one about the nun, the bishop and the donkey? You tell him your days of debating with Jehovah's Witnesses are long since over and attempt to close the door.

The door, of course, doesn't shut properly. This is because, as usual, Pisces is lying, literally as well as metaphysically, underneath it. He declares his undying love and swears he won't ever leave you again. However, this doesn't hold water since you hadn't actually noticed he'd left in the first place.

Oblivious to his bleats and yelps – you think it's the wind chimes – you trip over him, pick yourself up, dust him off and happily meander off into the library where you blithely bump into fellow Aquarius who's reading a book to try and impress you. Whereby you take the second volume of *The Life and Good Times of Sigmund Freud* (he's hogged volume one) and decide that discussing the meaning of sex with someone who doesn't deserve to have one is a complete waste of energy.

Instead you have a brainwave. Sick of not having a love life because you never seem to meet any men, you decide to discover the inner brazen hussy within and join the local knitting group.

The Pisces Goddess

20 February–20 March

The bastards are already forming a queue outside your door and we haven't even started yet. You do realise you're their last chance, don't you? How appropriate, then, that you're the only girl in the zodiac who can handle them all.

One bat of an eyelash and Aries will come, swinging out of a tree. You'll say 'Me Jane, who you?' so sweetly he'll promptly start beating up other large primates and gathering bananas to impress you. And somehow you'll manage to look impressed. You'll even be able to tell him how big and strong he is without losing your lunch.

Hold out your little finger and Leo will wrap himself around it. But he won't stay there for very long as you'd then have to contort yourself to worship at his feet. Make him understand you've been waiting to be his handmaid all your life and you'll not only get approval but him as well. To keep, forever. Are you sure you know what you're doing?

Act dumber than *he* is and Sagittarius will come galloping in. Tell him you aren't looking to tie him down; you'd be happy to see him whenever he breezes through town as being with him part time is better than being with another bastard full time (no choking), all the while gazing at him as if he's on the verge of saying something wise.

One look into your eyes and Cancer will be an incoherent mess on the floor. Oh, sorry – our mistake – he already was an incoherent mess on the floor. But you'll treat him as though he's capable of independent thought and action and help him to stand on his feet, causing him to feel the unfamiliar sensation of not hating himself which he naturally confuses with love for you.

Smile at Virgo and he'll begin to have romantic thoughts, though not exactly about sweeping you off your feet – more like sweeping around your feet. Be sweet and kind and pretend his retentiveness is a desirable masculine trait. And, hardest of all, try to look interested when he speaks.

Be coy around Gemini and he'll feel something in the void inside his chest go pitter-pat (probably a moth escaping). Hang on to every word he utters without making any demands or saying anything yourself and you'll experience something the rest of us have only had nightmares about – his undivided attention.

Look fragile and helpless; a look you first perfected in the cradle, and Taurus appears to ask if he can take care of you.

Show yourself to be happy to give up all your human rights in order to cook and he'll be eating out of your hand with alarming regularity.

Then pretend you can't make a decision to save your life and Libra will come out in sympathy. Convince him he's the most decisive man you've ever encountered and he'll begin to think you're the girl he's been waiting for through his three marriages and 62 relationships – not including the one-night stands.

Brush past Scorpio and he'll have his usual dark and sordid thoughts. Look as easy to manipulate as possible and play right into his hands. Go willingly to his little place in Hades and pretend the fire and brimstone furnishings would suit you to the ground (though even you can't pretend you're not a little worried about the neighbours).

Whilst living in purgatory, be unable to balance your cheque book and ask Capricorn to advise you. (Due to some of his business dealings he makes regular visits to hell.) Widen your eyes in amazement at his depth of knowledge on the subject and force yourself to giggle girlishly at all his little accounting jokes. Go on, tell him he's *funny* – he won't even bother to check your net worth.

Turn to Aquarius with your 'you're so [insert complimentary-masculine-sounding-adjective here]' routine and find he falls for it as easily as his shallower bastard friends despite all he preaches about quality and human dignity.

Take everything Pisces tells you as the gospel. Believe him wholeheartedly when he says he didn't know how that earring-that-wasn't-yours got into his bed. Tell him he is the most trustworthy man you have ever met – and he'll be pathetic enough to think you mean it.

How to Spot a B*st*rd by his Star Sign

Well, that was easy. Now you've got every bastard waiting, hoping you'll choose him. They all think they've found the perfect girl for them (naturally none of them are intelligent enough to realise things will change once the vows are made). But don't feel pressured into making a quick decision. As far as we're concerned you're quite welcome to the lot of them.